I'M A NOBODY

(But not to God)

Gregory M. Hasty

Copyright © 2022 Gregory M. Hasty.

All rights reserved. No part of this book may be used or reproduced by any means, graphic, electronic, or mechanical, including photocopying, recording, taping or by any information storage retrieval system without the written permission of the author except in the case of brief quotations embodied in critical articles and reviews.

This book is a work of non-fiction. Unless otherwise noted, the author and the publisher make no explicit guarantees as to the accuracy of the information contained in this book and in some cases, names of people and places have been altered to protect their privacy.

Archway Publishing books may be ordered through booksellers or by contacting:

Archway Publishing
1663 Liberty Drive
Bloomington, IN 47403
www.archwaypublishing.com
844-669-3957

Because of the dynamic nature of the Internet, any web addresses or links contained in this book may have changed since publication and may no longer be valid. The views expressed in this work are solely those of the author and do not necessarily reflect the views of the publisher, and the publisher hereby disclaims any responsibility for them.

Any people depicted in stock imagery provided by Getty Images are models, and such images are being used for illustrative purposes only. Certain stock imagery © Getty Images.

Interior Image Credit: Gregory M. Hasty

Scripture quotations taken from The Holy Bible, New International Version® NIV® Copyright © 1973 1978 1984 2011 by Biblica, Inc. TM. Used by permission. All rights reserved worldwide.

ISBN: 978-1-6657-1681-9 (sc)
ISBN: 978-1-6657-1680-2 (hc)
ISBN: 978-1-6657-1682-6 (e)

Library of Congress Control Number: 2021925642

Print information available on the last page.

Archway Publishing rev. date: 02/10/2022

CONTENTS

Dedication vii
Introduction ix
Chapter 1　Optimizing Your Optimism 1
Chapter 2　Absolutely Positively Good 11
Chapter 3　Don't Worry, Be Happy 17
Chapter 4　Hold on Just a Minute 29
Chapter 5　Pride Burns Brightly 37
Chapter 6　What's That I Hear? 45
Chapter 7　The Vanishing Art of Forgiveness 49
Chapter 8　Why Are Difficult People so Difficult? 56
Chapter 9　Gossip 66
Chapter 10　May I See Your ID, Please? 67
Chapter 11　One Step Removed from Our Comfort Zones ... 73
Chapter 12　Puzzle Paradox 80
Chapter 13　Ground Control to Father God, Can You Hear Us? ... 82
Chapter 14　Dear God, Do You Want to Go Steady? 91
Chapter 15　Ain't No Doubt 97

Chapter 16	Give It Up; It's Not Ours Anyway	104
Chapter 17	Heavens to Murgatroyd	111
Chapter 18	Calling All Angels	120
Chapter 19	Devil's in the Details	128
Chapter 20	Sin City	137
Chapter 21	Miracles Falling from Above	144
Chapter 22	Who's Foolin' Whom?	150
Chapter 23	Food for Thought	159
Chapter 24	Idol Time	166
Chapter 25	In Union We Stand; in Division We Fail	171
Chapter 26	What Really Matters	178
Afterword: The Reckoning		185
Acknowledgments		187
Sources		199

DEDICATION

I'm a Nobody was written in dedication to The Eagles. The Eagles are young students from villages in Costa Rica who are seeking to improve their education. The goal is to attend enhanced school programs and distance themselves from the drugs and violence in their village. To do so requires funds to pay for housing and tuition costs. One hundred percent of the net proceeds from *I'm a Nobody* will be donated to the eager students who await assistance. Never have I seen such a thirst to better themselves than the young men and women of Costa Rica.

INTRODUCTION

I'm not a theologian. Nor am I a seminary graduate with in-depth training in scripture, God, or religion. I have no certificates, degrees, or any time spent in the pulpit. You wouldn't recognize my name or find much about me on Google. I'm really just a nobody.

Jesus used a despised tax collector by the name of Matthew to serve as a disciple to spread the good news of His coming. God sent the prophet Samuel to approach a commonplace Jewish family, and He chose David, only a boy, rather than any of his older brothers to rule the Lord's kingdom. Moses was a reluctant orphan, selected to lead the Israelites out of Egypt, and Peter, the foundation of the Christian church, was an ordinary fisherman. So if these men were given opportunities with their vague résumés, it stands to reason God wouldn't mind if I wrote a book about Him.

Sometimes a layperson who stands on the outside looking in can provide a unique perspective that the ordinary Christian can relate to. We all go through moments of doubt and look to Jesus and the church for direction, each in our own way. Therefore, it's beneficial to hear new concepts and conclusions in order to fully discern our personal beliefs as they refine and mature. *I'm a Nobody* celebrates the individual who has fought his or her way into the fraternity of faith, regardless of the road taken to get there. Additionally, these writings are an invitation to those who have yet to find the peace of knowing and loving God. The goal of the following chapters is to raise the awareness of those who are followers so that they can continue to grow in their conviction and also for those who are just beginning their journeys.

God is complicated. He's elusive in His mystical being, and His actions are difficult to predict with any logical accuracy. He has a divine agenda beyond the furthest reaches of anyone's comprehension, like trying to understand how and where the universe ends or what eternal life may look like. If our Lord were predictable, and we understood the game plan and the results, why would we need Him? No doubt, we wouldn't. In the following pages, we explore the enigmas that remain impenetrable with hopes of unraveling the knots of these perceived mysteries. We often tend to overthink the concepts of faith and worship, and that's why the notions presented here attempt to boil things down to their simplest terms.

As you're reading the text, note that the chapters have a common theme that focuses on mental awareness and discipline. Without these two pillars of reasoning, it makes becoming a mature Christian very difficult. As our faith evolves, it accentuates the need for hyperawareness in everything we say and do. This acute *awareness* is essential in carrying out a righteous life. However, if we discard *discipline*, it renders awareness ineffective. We should employ this awareness, couple it with discipline, and watch how things start to bear fruit. Becoming a Christian requires effort. Discipline necessitates mental exertion. Controlling our actions, after all, can be a challenging task.

The first three chapters take us through physical and intellectual challenges dealing with optimism, developing a positive attitude and how to combat worry and anxiety. Once you get through the scientific and technical exploration of these attributes, the following chapters are less cognitively demanding and discuss the everyday challenges of patience, how to rein in your pride, forgiveness, gossip, and how to deal with difficult people. Are we a giver or a taker? Chapter 10 explores these traits and differentiates the two. This is followed by how to get to know God and ways to go about communicating with the Lord. We then examine doubt, followed by learning ways to be generous.

Ever want to know more about heaven, angels, the devil, sin or miracles? The succeeding chapters delve into these sometimes mysterious topics. Subsequent chapters introduce insightful discussions on what constitutes a fool, the importance of meals, fasting, idols and how essential corporate worship is to our walk in faith. The book ends with a personal perspective on what lives matter in our society today.

Find out if you're up to the challenge and have what it takes to be a Christian. This process is not for wimps. It's only for those who are able to keep their bodies under control and dictate how they should respond to the world's challenges. What faith is not, is letting your body control your mind. It's time we use our intellect to be in command so we can navigate our lives, not vice versa. If you've had enough of being pushed around by Satan, withering to his temptations, this book is for you. It will provide you with the stamina and the arsenal necessary to defeat the enemy and gain self-respect in the process.

It becomes clear over time that mastering our thoughts and behaviors is an indication of spiritual maturity. I pray that *I'm a Nobody* will shine a light on the path to righteousness and inspire readers to grow closer to God. Then pass it on to others and share the message.

Just remember *nobody* is a nobody. You have been and will always remain a special somebody to God.

CHAPTER 1
Optimizing Your Optimism

I'VE ALWAYS BEEN an optimist at heart. Not sure why. It's possibly tucked inside an individual DNA molecule within the nano-patterned substrate somewhere. Not that I know what that is exactly. Suffice it to say that's just the way we were built. Some say we were either born with it or not. A study of five hundred pairs of twins—one half reared together and the other half separated early in life—found that optimism was inherited approximately 25 percent of the time. "But then the rest is shaped by stuff that happens to you across your life," said William Chopik, assistant professor at Michigan State University. He went on to say it may depend on, "Your parents, how did they treat you? How did your relationships with your friends go? Are you a good student? Did you experience a lot of success early in life?" He coauthored another study looking at 75,000 people, including 22,150 Americans from ages 18 to 104. It found there are other factors that might influence the optimism trait, such as where we are on the age spectrum: "optimism generally increases throughout younger adulthood, flattens out between about ages 55 and 70, then decreases again after that." Chopik further remarked, "As a teenager or college student you look ahead, then you form a family, develop hobbies and find excitement in life. As we age, individuals 'get better at stuff' we become more competent, which gives us confidence and optimism." Then Professor Chopik says, "Once poor health and other limitations of age start appearing, optimism plateaus and eventually starts to decline."[1]

Are We an Optimist?

This attitude called optimism can be found somewhere in our mental premises, and as stated, it depends on factors related to our genetics, childhood, consequences of life, and age. If optimism isn't conspicuous, can it be acquired? There are, in fact, ways to enhance this characteristic as part of one's personal resources. Let's find out how by first determining the current state of our optimism. Do we expect more good things to happen than bad, or do we rarely count on good things to happen? If we're described by the former, we're trending toward being optimists. If the second example describes us more accurately, yes, we may in fact be pessimists. If we're classified as pessimists, it may be time to wield the scalpel and insert an implant of optimism. As a willing patient, relax and be anesthetized by the Holy Spirit until the procedure is complete.

The apostle Paul writes in Romans 15:13, "May the God of hope fill you with all joy and peace as you trust in him, so that you may overflow with hope by the power of the Holy Spirit."

The Progression of Hope to Optimism

Hope is defined, "as a feeling of expectation and desire for a certain thing to happen."[2] The definition of optimism is, "hopefulness and confidence about the future or the successful outcome of something."[3]

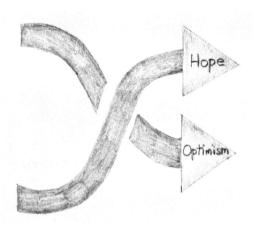

Based on the two definitions, hope and optimism are closely aligned. The word "optimism" isn't mentioned anywhere in the 1,189 chapters of the Bible; however, the feeling of optimism isn't a new concept. It's an emotion that's been around since humankind was created. Buying in to this premise, we can presume that if we're *hopeful*, there's a good chance we'll be *optimistic* as well.

According to Helen Keller, "Optimism is the faith that leads to achievement. Nothing can be done without hope and confidence."[4] Ms. Keller used two compelling words in her sixteen-word quote: "faith" and "hope." If anyone knows about optimism, it would be Helen Keller. After losing both her sight and hearing as an infant, she called on her optimism to flourish and became a writer, author, and proponent for people with disabilities. Remarkably, Helen Keller was the first deaf-blind person to earn a BA degree.[5] She could have grumbled and stewed in her misery for being shortchanged out of arguably the two most critical sensory elements a human can possess. But she didn't.

Taking it a step further, Rebecca Bloom said, "I think I am going to have to supercharge my optimism to arm myself for the battle ahead."[6] Ms. Bloom's term "supercharge" may well provide some insight to our discussions in solving the undertaking. How might one go about the supercharging process? Here are a few power sources.

SUPERCHARGE BY SCRIPTURE

The Bible gives us hope; it lets us in on a secret—the secret of eternal life. Knowing that there's something waiting for us after death helps us exude optimism for something that is certain, even though our brains fall short of understanding exactly how it works. "Now faith is being sure of what we hope for and certain of what we do not see" (Hebrews 11:1).

Having faith kindles hope. Hope in turn spawns optimism.

> "For I know the plans I have for you," declares the Lord, plans to prosper you and not to harm you, plans to give you hope and a future (Jeremiah 29:11).

Some may question the use of scripture as a basis to finding hope. The Bible is merely words written in a book, one might argue. How and why should we rely on these assurances to provide hope and optimism? Responding to these claims, the Bible is the most read book in the world. It has sold more copies in the last fifty years than any other book, estimated at over 3.9 billion. Its origin dates back thousands of years. Then it could be asked, is the Bible still relevant today? The most brilliant minds in the world couldn't dispel its accuracy, and it survived countless translations, keeping the Bible's messages intact. It recounts what eyewitnesses saw and experienced before Jesus was born and afterward. Scripture tells the story of creation, God, His people, and His only offspring, Jesus. The Bible is viewed as authentic because of its historical accuracy, its undeniable longevity, and a belief that God inspired the authors who wrote the verses. If the Bible can't be considered reliable and historically accurate, why has it been memorized, documented, translated, and reproduced over the last two thousand years?

Some of the available history involving the circumstances around Jesus's time is credited to a man named Flavius Josephus. Fortunately, he was born around AD 37, soon after Jesus was crucified. Before becoming a renowned historian, he was a commander of the Jewish forces in Galilee and would later become a Roman citizen. Josephus was employed by the Flavian emperors Vespasian, Titus, and Domitian to chronicle the events of their time. His writings were considered accurate and reliable, which made Josephus a trusted authority by most scholars for historical archives during this period. Although there is some debate about the early historian's account in *Testimonium Flavianum* declaring Jesus as the Messiah, the interpretation is still believed by many.[7]

When we rely on Josephus's accounts, like so many have over the last twenty centuries, it's one more assurance that the Bible is accurate. Facts found in the Bible are supported by the many individuals who saw and personally experienced the accounts between Genesis and Revelation. So the first principle to supercharging our optimism is a healthy dose of scriptural inspiration. By absorbing the verses, we can begin to develop faith and hope. The advent of hope triggers the barometer that measures optimism, then trends upward, giving us a fighting chance to persevere in this strange, challenging world of ours.

SUPERCHARGE BY PROTECTING THE TEMPLE

> Do you not know that your body is a temple of the Holy Spirit, who is in you, whom you have received from God? You are not your own; you were bought at a price. Therefore honor God with your body. (1 Corinthians 6:19–20)

The above verses from Corinthians help us understand that the body is God's unique creation. There's no other like it, no two alike. God not only wants, but insists that we take care of our bodies. The temple He created is His. We are merely a caretaker of the physical unit that houses our mind and soul while temporarily marooned on earth. That's why it's imperative we safeguard His spiritual design by putting good things into it. Alcohol, tobacco, drugs, poisons, and radiation are but a few things we regularly introduce into His work of art. Besides doing physical harm by ingesting or exposing ourselves to these common offerings, they negatively affect our mental well-being too. If we truly desire to be optimistic, we need to quit poisoning our bodies. Feed it the right foods, and kick the toxins to the curb. If it's not obvious what we should be eating, we need to find out. B. K. S. Iyengar says it succinctly: "Health is a state of complete harmony of the body, mind and spirit."[8] When one of the three elements is out of sync, we lose harmony. If we're not personally in harmony, it will be that much harder to be in harmony with God. It's certainly possible to subsist on two of the three elements—many of us do—but it's not optimal.

When driving a car and one tire goes flat, it halts progress. The car doesn't drive properly because it has lost one of its four fundamental components. The three essential determinants mentioned above by Iyengar work in union to develop harmony. When one is not present, it disrupts what would otherwise be a well-oiled machine. The body is the custodian of the mind and the spirit; it's the workhorse of the triumvirate. When our outer anatomy fails, the other two elements are trapped inside and suffer the body's fate. God gave us rational thinking so that we can make corrections when our bodily equipment isn't working properly. We need to use this intelligence to safeguard our temples so that they can function like they were designed. Imagine when we get to heaven and encounter the gatekeeper who's wearing his green visor and checking notes on a clipboard. He scrolls down to find a line item on the spreadsheet that asks, "Did this person take care of God's temple while on earth?" How would we answer?

Supercharge with Supplementation

Aside from the contaminants mentioned earlier, it's recognized that food today lacks the nutritional value it once contained. Furthermore. many of the groceries we buy can be detrimental to our health, and fast food is closer to poison than nutrition. This makes supplements absolutely essential, and it's so important for us to read labels. Learn what to avoid. Read www.drhyman.com or www.wellandgood.com to find out which essential supplements shore up the shortfalls in our diet. Even if we eat a completely well-rounded, healthy diet, we'll still be deficient in some areas. Why not build an arsenal of strength around our physical castle. Supplements are our turrets, moats, ramparts, and battlements when our bodies are under siege. Make it a harder for bad food and toxins to storm the walls. To create harmony, eat wisely, add supplements, and take the vitamins Mahailia recommends below.

> Faith and prayer are the vitamins of the soul; man cannot live in health without them. (Mahailia Jackson[9])

Supercharge by Fitness

We can eat properly, take our supplements, add faith and prayer as vitamins, but there's still something missing. God's temple is a mechanism that requires movement to burn calories. Our body needs more than eating responsibly; it needs to spend energy. The body's pistons need to be turning for the train to move efficiently down the track. Podcaster, writer, and movement coach Brock Armstrong says,

> Exercise affects the brain in many ways. It increases heart rate, which pumps more oxygen to the brain. It aids the release of hormones which provides an excellent environment for the growth of brain cells. Exercise also promotes brain plasticity by stimulating growth of new connections between cells in many important cortical areas of the brain. Research from UCLA even demonstrated that exercise increased growth factors in the brain which makes it easier for the brain to grow new neuronal connections.[10]

We should be able to connect the dots to see a correlation between a healthy brain and optimism. Armstrong goes on to say,

> From a more feel-good perspective, the same antidepressant-like effects associated with the "runner's high" has been correlated with a drop in stress hormones. A study from Stockholm showed that the antidepressant effect of running was also associated with more cell growth in the hippocampus, an area of the brain responsible for learning and memory. The study went as far as to say "Thus, suppression of cell proliferation in the hippocampus

could constitute one of the mechanisms that underlie depression, and physical activity might be an efficient antidepressant."[11]

We don't necessarily have to be a jogger or runner to feel the same effects. Biking, walking, weights, tennis, and swimming are all ways to stimulate the brain and feed it the essentials to operate at maximum efficiency. Crystal Fenton, whose article in *Spirituality & Health* quotes Dr. Michael Okun, a professor at University of Florida Health and is also the national medical director of the National Parkinson Foundation, says, "Many people believe that physical exercise as well as mental exercise and engagement will be the key to living long, healthy and meaningful lives with top-notch brain function. Exercise every day. Exercise is like a drug; it leads to the release of neurotropic factors which are like the brain's miracle grow."[12]

There's only one way to experience the difference, and that's to exercise and feel the endorphins erupting inside.

> The cheerful mind perseveres, and the strong mind hews its way through a thousand difficulties. (Swami Vivekananda[13])

The formula for optimizing our optimism is:

1. Scriptural cliff diving into the Bible.
2. Put good food in the trough.
3. Move the bones around.

> The essence of optimism is that it takes no account of the present, but it is a source of inspiration, of vitality and hope where others have resigned; it enables a man to hold his head high, to claim the future for

himself and not to abandon it to his enemy. (Dietrich Bonhoeffer[14])

Optimism is the madness of insisting that all is well when we are miserable. (Voltaire[15])

Dear Father God, we want to be optimistic. Guide our words from negativity. May we hold our tongues from words that don't honor you. Feed us this formula to bolster our optimism. Amen.

CHAPTER 2
Absolutely Positively Good

HAVING A POSITIVE attitude is a by-product of optimism. It may be difficult to distinguish between the two until we examine words closely and note the similarities. We've already concluded that optimism is *hopefulness and confidence about the future or the successful outcome of something.* A positive attitude is *a state of mind that envisions and expects favorable results.* Based on chapter 1 conclusions, it can be said that optimism is an internal feeling manufactured by forces within our intellects. It's a psychological, intrinsic emotion. So how does this differ from a positive attitude?

Optimism's Transformation into a Positive Attitude

Optimism is a cognitive function that expresses how a person feels about himself and the future. A positive attitude is a reflection of that feeling. In essence, optimism engenders a positive attitude, which is displayed in our behaviors to those around us. The general term "attitude" means, "a settled way of thinking or feeling about someone or something, typically one that is reflected in a person's behavior."[16]

The first half of the definition talks about feelings (cognitive). The remainder changes course and indicates how our behaviors are reflected (physical). Said in layperson's terms, it's the way we act and how our thoughts affect what we do and say. So optimism is most certainly a stimulus for a positive attitude.

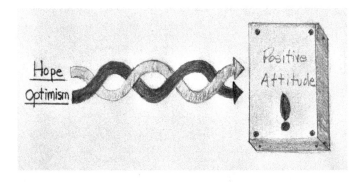

Following the progression, we can say reading scripture and taking care of our earthly anatomy via diet, supplements and exercise give birth to optimism. As our intellect forms optimism, a positive attitude emerges. Even though the two are different, the recipe for optimism is also a formula for a positive attitude as Armstrong emphasizes throughout his studies. It's fascinating to talk with runners and joggers. They seem to have a pleasant disposition, lots of energy, bright eyes, and an optimistic perspective on life. We like to be around these individuals. They inspire us to feel good, and we can sense their energy. Runners are somehow able to attract positive vibes floating around the invisible slipstream and weave them into their personas. This is not unlike faithful Christians. We can feel spiritual energy and positivity exuding from a Christian's disposition. In the case of a runner, the physical exertion creates a chemical release within the brain, resulting in optimism and hence, a positive attitude. From the Christian's perspective, hope is generated by faith from reading scripture and worshipping God. The believer is similar to the runner where optimism is expressed by the person's attitude and behavior. If a Christian is operating on only two of the three Iyengar tenants (mind and spirit), imagine the potential if meaningful exercise and healthy eating were added.

> When you are joyful, when you say yes to life and have fun and project positivity all around you, you become a sun in the center of every constellation, and people want to be near you. (Shannon L. Alder[17])

> Don't hang with negative people. They will pull you down with them. Instead, invite them into your light and together you will both shine strong. (L. F. Young[18])

THE ENERGY OF A POSITIVE ATTITUDE

Who comes to mind when discussing a positive attitude? The first person that jumps to the forefront is a man I heard speak several times. He was born prematurely in Alabama, the tenth of twelve children. He was the youngest of all the boys. His father died of a stroke when he was six. Two days later, a younger sister passed away. Not the ideal childhood. He fought through adversity and grew up working on a farm, eventually finding his way into college, but later dropped out. He became a salesman and excelled to astonishing levels. After his phenomenal career in corporate America, he became a motivational speaker and author.[19] His name is probably familiar, Zig Ziglar. His positivity is renown. Confidence and exuberance sprang from his disposition like a water-stressed spillway. Ziglar's positive attitude attracted businesses from all over the world who solicited his advice, energy, and positive mindset. He ranks up there with some of the most influential individuals of our time, and he enhanced thousands of lives. His philosophy centered around, "I've always believed that when something happens to you that you don't like, you can either respond, which is positive, or you can react, which is negative."[20]

Ziglar found his faith at age forty-five and was a strong Christian man. His faith was the cornerstone of his energy, enthusiasm, and positive thinking. He often said so. "Life is too short to spend your precious time trying to convince a person who wants to live in gloom and doom otherwise. Give lifting that person your best shot, but don't hang around long enough for his/her bad attitude to pull you down. Instead, surround yourself with optimistic people."[21]

Many people found themselves drawn to Ziglar and others like him. The man's charisma and energy were alluring, and his influence was widespread. People who follow his teachings develop a positive attitude that boosts self-confidence, and they make a significant impact on all they meet. Ziglar engendered hope, optimism, and an enthusiastic attitude.

RIPPLE EFFECT

Our actions can impact hundreds if not thousands of people in a lifetime. It's impossible to know who might be observing our actions. We should demonstrate the right attitude so others can emulate the positive examples we set. These influences have a ripple effect that can play forward to children, adults, family members, even people we don't know. Attitudes cross over generational timelines and can be an inheritance to those who follow.

The Bible says, "Finally, brothers, whatever is true, whatever is noble, whatever is right, whatever is pure, whatever is lovely, whatever is admirable—if anything is excellent or praiseworthy—think about such things" (Philippians 4:8 NIV).

And, "Do not let any unwholesome talk come out of your mouths, but only what is helpful for building others up according to their needs, that it may benefit those who listen" (Ephesians 4:29).

Optimism in Action

Optimism that is constructed by faith and supplemented with good health and eating habits can't help but create a positive attitude. A good way to begin the journey is to start the morning with positive thoughts. As we swing those tired legs over the side of the bed, think how nice it is to be alive and the opportunity and excitement that awaits. Leave stress and dread tucked under the pillow. As the day presents its challenges, meet them head-on, and use each obstacle as a learning opportunity to better ourselves in some way.

I'm reminded of the story of a man who was standing on a street corner when a car drove up and the tire accidentally rolled over his foot. A fellow pedestrian looked at him with pity and expressed her sympathy for such a painful ordeal. He looked over at her, forced a smile and said, "It hurts now, but I'm gonna feel so much better when it rolls off." Now that's a positive attitude!

We should find humor in situations that are unfavorable. It's much easier to laugh at our circumstances so that we can focus on what good will come out of the experience. Turn mistakes and failures into life lessons. All missteps offer wisdom. We should challenge ourselves to say only positive things. When we find negative words forming in our minds, capture the thoughts before they leave, then reconstruct the mental message into a more-appropriate response. Words escaping the mouth are like toothpaste squeezed from a tube. Once it's out, it's impossible to put back.

Let's surround ourselves with those who are positive and affirm our ideals. Like Zig Ziglar recommends, don't let pessimists drag us down. Refine the art of avoiding those who want to pull us into the quagmire, yet accept the challenge to lift them up. There are no dead ends, only diversions. When problems arise, offer solutions. Help someone have a good day.

As we plow the rows of life, it's important to remember speaking of ourselves in uplifting terms. The more we put ourselves down, the more we'll begin thinking in those terms. Our mind hears what we say. Concentrate on being a positive charge on the battery of life. Don't be a scowling, downtrodden, unpleasant character everyone avoids.

Dear Lord, give us the strength to be positive. Help us to ignore distractions that would rob us of our happiness. Amen.

CHAPTER 3

Don't Worry, Be Happy

Therefore I tell you, do not worry about your life, what you will eat or drink; or about your body, what you will wear. Is not life more important than food, and the body more important than clothes? Look at the birds of the air; they do not sow or reap or store away in barns, and yet your heavenly Father feeds them. Are you not much more valuable than they? Who of you by worrying can add a single hour to his life?

—Matthew 6:25–27

THIS CHAPTER FOCUSES on the enigma of worry, stress, and anxiety. Here we embark on an odyssey to understand how worry and anxiety find their way into our minds. From a scientific perspective we'll explore, how the body addresses these emotions. We can then learn ways to cope with these perplexing maladies.

What Are Worry and Anxiety?

Worry and anxiety are interchangeable although not identical, similar to comparing optimism and a positive attitude discussed earlier. What constitutes a worrier or someone who has anxiety? Does one constantly fear the unknown or become overly concerned with what tomorrow will bring? How about stressing over the economy, pandemics, political turmoil, family, general health, or personal safety? This is not uncommon; we all tend to worry. This wretch called worry is programmed into the software of our psyches.

We think of the feeling of worry as showing uneasiness or anxiety, and dwelling on troubles. Taking this baseline meaning, it suggests that our brains manufacture worry which is triggered by various types of external stimulation. Anxiety, on the other hand, is a feeling of worry, nervousness, or unease about an imminent event or something with an uncertain outcome. Therefore, when worry surfaces, it manifests into anxiety, causing unease, dread, and distress.

> Therefore do worry about tomorrow, for tomorrow will worry about itself. Each day has enough trouble of its own. (Matthew 6:34)

In our fast-paced society fueled by social media and the ability to communicate instantaneously, it's a fact we're constantly bombarded with information. Shrouded within the avalanche of information are things that make us worry. This external stimulation can most often be attributed to the media. The communication industry thrives, and can only exist, by reporting stories that stimulate some reaction within the minds of its listeners. As a human weakness, we've developed the uncanny thirst for stories that are shocking, sensational, or have some degree of intrigue. We easily get bored hearing good news or anything that's pedestrian or commonplace. So the media spoon-feeds us what we crave, but in the process, catalyzes an unwanted stimulation within our psyches. Yes, worry. For a viewer watching news channels all day long, it's a sure bet this person has developed a supercharged case of anxiety.

Besides the media, there are other factors that can make us anxious. Mental or physical trauma can cause similar feelings. Some examples are violence, verbal and physical abuse, bullying, isolation, abandonment, death of a loved one, accidents, or plain old bad luck. Each can be a fountainhead for worry.

Homeostasis

We are all worriers at times. Even when things are okay, we're still able to manufacture a worry of some kind. Why? What causes this affliction? As we analyze the effects of media stimulation and its barrage of information, and the long-term consequences of mental trauma, it warrants a pathological examination. What we seek as individuals, whether we're aware of it or not, is homeostasis. This is the internal balance of our bodies' mechanisms or the stability of our physiological states. Homeostasis seeks a metabolic equilibrium between two chemical forces, that of *stimulating* and *tranquilizing*. Worry and anxiety disturb this balance. Science shows:

> When you encounter a stressor—whether it's an angry bear or an unreasonable deadline—a chain of events kicks off in your brain. First, the amygdala, an area of your brain that processes emotion, gets information about the stressor through your senses. If it interprets that information as something

threatening or dangerous, it sends a signal to your brain's command center, known as the hypothalamus. When your hypothalamus gets a signal from your amygdala that you're in danger, it sends signals to the adrenal glands and activates your sympathetic nervous system. The adrenals pump out adrenaline, causing your heart to beat faster, forcing more blood into your muscles and organs. Next, the hypothalamus activates a network called the HPA axis, which is made up of the hypothalamus, pituitary, and adrenals. This can cause these areas to release more stress hormones, including cortisol, which forces your body to stay wired and alert.[22]

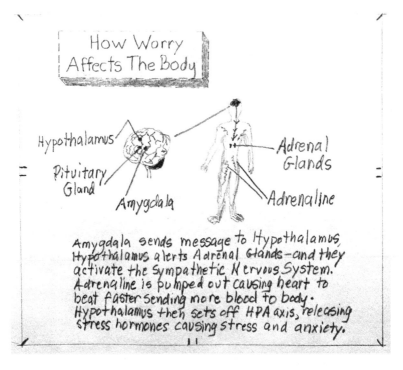

This article, quoted by WebMD, goes on to say that when stress hormones are released, many short- and long-term detrimental effects can occur. This includes the musculoskeletal, respiratory, and cardiovascular systems, all of which can be negatively impacted. As worry and anxiety take control of our senses, it creates an imbalance. Homeostasis is disrupted. If we happen to be a consistent worrier, even about routine events and activities, it will trip the circuit breaker and interrupt homeostasis. In extreme cases, some individuals demonstrate conditions known as general anxiety disorder (GAD), which is a serious ailment that can lead to depression, isolation, and phobias. This also includes panic disorder and obsessive-compulsive disorder. "GAD patients reveal an unusual brain pattern where impulses are sent to the hippocampus but the lines of communication were muddled and had poor connectivity to parts of the brain responsible for determining the importance of an event or concern."[23] The bad news about this Stanford Medicine News Center report is that long-term stress, anxiety, and depression have been linked to an increased risk of dementia and Alzheimer's. Bottom line is that worry can affect our health, long-term viability, and quality of life.

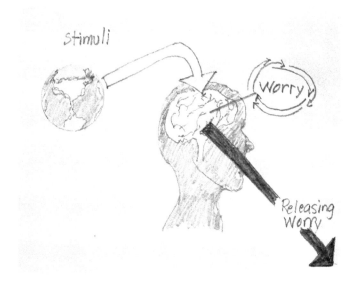

> As a rule, what is out of sight disturbs men's minds more seriously than what they see. (Julius Caesar[24])

What Does God Think about Worry?

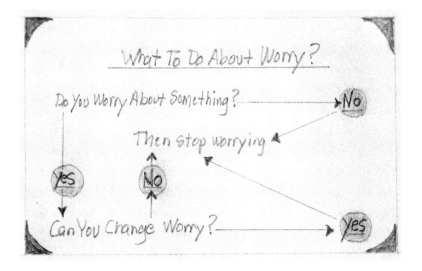

No one has faced more stress and nerve-racking anxiety than the apostle Paul. Shipwrecks, imprisonment, persecution, suffering, and his eventual crucifixion are examples. This man of God experienced every threat and consequence imaginable. If we were to ask someone's advice on how to handle worry, Paul should be our go-to for advice: "Do not be anxious about anything, but in everything, by prayer and petition, with thanksgiving, present your requests to God. And the peace of God, which transcends all understanding, will guard your hearts and your minds in Christ Jesus" (Philippians 4:6–7).

Paul didn't have the luxury of Google or the scientific knowledge we've learned over the centuries. However, Paul did know that worry impacts our *heart* and *mind*. In only two succinct sentences he gives us the prescription for curing worry and anxiety. Give our worries to

God. Our Father God does not like His children to worry. He not only disapproves of our worrying, He strongly discourages us from worrying. Why? Because worry is a sign that we don't trust Him. Sarah Young's book *Jesus Calling* has a vivid daily devotional with a poignant message concerning worry. So impressed with her interpretation of Luke 12:22–31 and John 16:33, I decided to print the text from her book, put it on a placard, and attach it to the wall of my office at work. It survived a company change from one fast-moving, stressful job to another and was a constant reminder, comforting me for over ten years. It drives home the point how God feels about worry. It's included here for insight on how to win the battle against worry and anxiety.

> I am all around you, like a cocoon of Light. My presence with you is a promise, independent of your awareness of Me. Many things can block this awareness, but the major culprit is worry. My children tend to accept worry as an inescapable fact of life. However, worry is a form of unbelief; it is anathema to Me.
>
> Who is in charge of your life? If it is you, then you have good reason to worry. But if it is I, then worry is both unnecessary and counterproductive. When you start to feel anxious about something, relinquish the situation to Me. Back off a bit, redirecting your focus to Me. I will either take care of the problem Myself or show you how to handle it. In this world you will have problems, but you need not lose sight of Me.[25]

Cycle of Stress

The following diagram is called the Cycle of Stress. It shows the twelve stages of stress overlaid on a diagram of a clock. Numbers 1 through 6 are designated as the "safe zone', that is, a particular worry hasn't risen to a level of concern. Numbers 4 through 6, however, are when a dilemma materializes, and worry begins to surface. It's recognized and raises uncertainty. Numbers 7 through 9 depart from the safe zone, and we find ourselves in the "danger zone." We become annoyed and anxious, and worry sets in. If anxiety escalates beyond this stage, it leads to anguish, stress, and finally panic. From what we've described earlier, numbers 10 through 12 are most likely where physical and mental suffering can occur; it is fittingly called the "damage area."

Ideally, we should remain in the safe zone when possible. It's virtually unthinkable to assume we can continually lounge comfortably on the right side of the circle with the notion we'll avoid crossing into the dreaded realm of 6 or higher. Knowing there will always be times we find ourselves between numbers 7 and 12, we should therefore devise a plan when crossing into this region. The plan for returning to the safe zone is our reliance on God. Once we cross into perilous realms, we should punt the ball to God, and make our way back to where we belong.

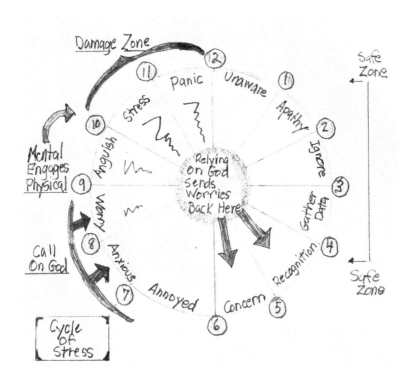

Surviving Stress

Eliminating worry is equivalent to having faith. Belief in God allows us the ability to pass the worry on to Him. When we find ourselves in the grasp of stress, or when we're worried or feel anxious, we should place our trust in the Lord. Once this is done, it prevents emotional damage to our bodies.

Another helpful approach is to be in communion with others. We should discuss our worries with trusted friends and seek advice and direction. We can also distract ourselves from the sources of stress by walking away. Avoid conflict and temptation, plan ahead, stay organized, and be under control. It's vital to steer clear of situations that put us in a stressful state. Lastly, as a reminder, we should take care of the body God entrusted to us. Eat right, get our eight hours, and exercise. The combination of entrusting our worries to God and taking care of what's under our control (the body) go a long way to neutralizing our worries.

Christian author and speaker Joanie Yoder was consumed with anxiety, stress, and worry. Ms. Yoder said that the greatest discovery we can make is to realize that our own strength is not enough. Her story is not unique: "My life was filled with anxiety and worry, but I was able to cover it up, like a lot of people do, until I had an experience that caused me to hit rock bottom. It was then that I was forced to face my anxieties, my fears, my dread, and my worries."

"I experienced that discovery. I had nothing left of my own inner resources. I didn't seem to have the strength, physically or emotionally, to go on.

> I had developed agoraphobia, which is a dread of open spaces—a fear of going out. For me, it was a fear of going into the supermarket. It was so intense that I would panic and go into a sweat. I was afraid that I would go totally insane in front of people—or, even worse, die.
>
> Sometimes I would interrupt my shopping, shove my cart into a corner, and run home. As soon as I was in the house, I had this sudden relief of being safe and secure again.
>
> I thought I was the only person who felt like this. My eating habits changed, my sleep was erratic, I was trembly and shaky, and I was generally anxious about life and all its responsibilities. I couldn't face

anything. I felt I was all washed up by the time I was in my early thirties.

There were underlying reasons for my difficulty. As I look back now, I realize that there were three reasons for my inability to manage life:

One was extreme immaturity. I was underdeveloped emotionally to handle responsibility.

Second, I had developed a bitterness habit. I didn't really recognize it as such, because I felt I was always justified in feeling as I did. Mine was always a just cause.

And the third reason, which I think is common to all of us, was a tendency to be self-sufficient. I tried to do everything in my own strength. And when I realized that I couldn't do it on my own, I felt I ought to be able to.

Those three factors had a crumbling effect. It led me toward a breakdown that I needed. I think it's a breakdown we all need. It wasn't a nervous breakdown, but a breakdown of my self-sufficiency.

From my own experience, and also in observing other people who are in this painful situation of running out of their resources, one of the characteristics is a need to control—the need to control life, circumstances, people, and unwittingly, God—because we feel afraid of what might happen. We feel that if we can control things and make things go a certain way, we will be less afraid."[26]

If you see ten troubles coming down the road, you can be sure that nine will run into the ditch before they reach you. (Calvin Coolidge[27])

For peace of mind, resign as general manager of the universe. (Larry Eisenberg[28])

If things go wrong, don't go with them. (Roger Babson[29])

Love looks forward, hate looks back, anxiety has eyes all over its head. (Mignon McLaughlin[30])

Worry is a thin stream of fear trickling through the mind. If encouraged, it cuts a channel into which all other thoughts are drained. (Arthur Somers Roche[31])

Every evening I turn my worries over to God. He's going to be up all night anyway. (Mary Crowley[32])

Dear heavenly Father, give us peace; calm our minds. When we feel worried, take it from our grasp. Amen.

CHAPTER 4

Hold on Just a Minute

BEFORE WE GET ahead of ourselves and hurry through this chapter, show a little patience. Give the words a chance to get comfortably seated before we start. This thing called patience is what most of us seek, but it is often in short supply.

One day I was stuck behind a long line of cars spread across three lanes at a traffic signal in my hometown of Plano, Texas. I was in the center lane. After the light cycled through a green light for the second time, my lane still didn't move. On either side of me the vehicles were able to drive forward without any delays and made it through the light. The reason my lane wasn't moving was because the driver in front of me wasn't moving. Inexplicably she was trying to shift over into the busy right lane, thus holding up traffic, not only in my lane, but the other as well. I became impatient (an under-exaggeration), and probably mumbled things under my breath I wouldn't be proud of discussing here. The second her rear bumper was out of my way, I hit the accelerator, trying to make the light before it changed again. Before I had time to react, my car ran over a big, fat cinderblock that appeared in the roadway which had been concealed by her car. It became painfully obvious the block was what obstructed the path of her car. My right front tire took the brunt of the impact and exploded. I sheepishly pulled into the lane she then occupied and found a place to exit. I stopped and changed the flat. Not one of my brighter moments.

This is not an isolated case. I've gotten into so many jams because of my impatience. My wife, Sue, often reminds me to take it easy. "Don't be hasty," she says. I swear it's in my DNA. It's also in my name, which at times I feel inclined to live up to. When sitting down to type this chapter, it came to me that I'm really writing these words to myself. Hopes are that by assembling thoughts about this elusive personality trait I will somehow pick up on some ideas to help my own affliction.

Patience Unwrapped

Patience is the ability to accept or tolerate delays, problems, or suffering without becoming annoyed or anxious. Sounds like the writer of this definition saw my faux pas at the traffic signal. It's clear to me now that I couldn't tolerate the delay. Nor was I able to contain my annoyance or anxiety. The word "patience" comes from the Greek word *Hypomone*, which means to remain under or to abide under.[33] Digging deeper, "Hypomone" was originally meant to bear up courageously under suffering.[34]

Sue should remind me when I get out of hand to be more hypomone; maybe that will register. Try as we may, patience is one of the hardest attributes to master. Especially in our give-it-to-me-now world we live in today. Strangely enough it seems like we encourage impatience nowadays. We want instantaneous information, gratification, and resolution. Patience is truly a lost competence and an abating characteristic, like trying to repair our own car.

Readings tell us that we should treat patience as if it were a muscle. Exercise it and watch it develop. The question remains how to flex this muscle before we instinctively react. When these situations arise, our predisposition to react usually takes precedence. We get antsy, and instead of using this elusive, phantom muscularity, we take the easy way out and react with impatience.

To better understand this mysterious muscle, let's break down the concept of patience into three components.

OPA

1. *Opportunity:* A patience opportunity arises when there's something we seek in the future, something that's delayed or hasn't happened yet. It could also be aggravation with people or time itself for moving too slowly or things not going how we would like them to. These situations activate the patience opportunity.

2. *Processing*: Once the opportunity presents itself, the brain processes the dilemma and decides what to do about it. We can choose how to react from a smorgasbord of options, like anger, frustration, disappointment, complaining, aggression, or some other reaction masquerading as impatience.

3. *Action*: The final element within the OPA composition is self-explanatory. We sense the opportunity, we process the options, then we act. Unfortunately, the problem for many of us, including yours truly, is that we bypass step 2. The situation presents itself, then we react. We don't take enough time to process or analyze the circumstances. It would do us all good to remember the acronym OPA whenever our patience is challenged: opportunity/process/act.

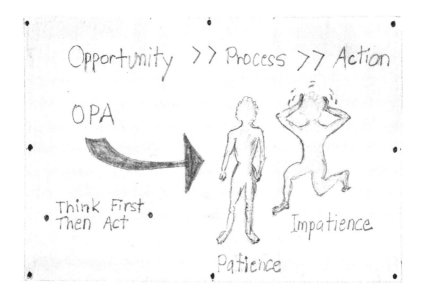

Proverbs 19:11 says, "A man's wisdom gives him patience; it is to his glory to overlook an offense." King Solomon explains that we should introduce wisdom before reacting. This novel concept fits perfectly into the realm of step 2 of the OPA, *processing*.

THOSE IN THE KNOW

Arguably the most influential Christian leader in the United States over the last century was Billy Graham. His perspectives and religious disciplines have enhanced so many lives over the years, including my own. What does he say about patience?

> It is the regular exercise of patience and long-suffering in the small day to day frustrations and irritations which prepares us to endure when the great battle comes. (Billy Graham[35])

As we learned in chapter 3, worrying has negative consequences on the body and mind. So does impatience, according to The Billy Graham Evangelist Association. They opine, "First of all it harms us physically, emotionally and spiritually. It also can harm our relationship with others. Impatience easily turns into anger or even violence, and these are the opposite of God's plan for us."[36]

Most incidents creating impatience occur when something happens over which we have no control. So if we can't do anything about it, why get upset? Simply realizing we can't change the situation may help us to relax and accept the circumstances. Refocusing for a moment on my incident at the signal light, I realize now the damage was caused by my lack of patience. It was swift and severe.

Joyce Meyer shares her wisdom: "Patience is not simply the ability to wait—it's how we behave while we're waiting."[37]

Biblical Patience

There are many characters in the Bible who exhibited patience, some quite obvious.

Moses

When first thinking about those in the Bible who exemplified patience, Moses was one of the first that came to mind. His story is wrought with continual patience. He didn't feel qualified to convince the Israelites to leave Egypt but was patient with God's commands and followed through with his Lord's instruction. Moses wasn't confident about his speaking abilities, but again was patient, and accepted God's plan to work with his older brother Aaron on his behalf. He patiently shepherded the Israelites through the desert, waiting for the right time to enter the land of milk and honey. For forty years! Forty years—now that's patience. He did this knowing he'd never inherit the Promised Land.

Job

Job is certainly the epitome of patience when this concept is envisioned. Think of the colloquialism, "The patience of Job". It has survived for hundreds of years, so there must be something to it. I've heard this phrase many a time. God saw Job as a man who was deserving, upright and faithful. Because of a confrontation between God and Satan, Job became the unknowing participant in a challenge to test his faith. God told Satan that Job would persevere through any hardships that were cast upon him. Satan wagered against him. Job proceeded to weather the storm from attacks on his livelihood, his family, and finally even his physical health. Time after time Job was smitten with loss, disappointment and temptation, unthinkable burdens. Rather than give in and curse God—which is what Satan was angling for—he stayed the course. He was patient and waited for the Lord's deliverance. God did deliver, and Job's patience was rewarded. If you haven't read this inspiring account in the Old Testament, the Book of Job is an eye-opener. Even if you have, it is worth reading again for inspiration.

Abraham and Sarah

Abraham and Sarah are good examples of both patience and impatience. God promised the couple they would have descendants as numerous as the stars. The problem was, they couldn't have children in their early years. Then they grew too old to bear offspring. The two heard God's promise, but as they were processing their patience opportunity, they gave in to impatience when Sarah suggested to Abraham to have children with her handmaid, Hagar. They succumbed to the temptation due to their restlessness, and a son was born named Ishmael. Was this a good decision? Apparently not because Ishmael was ground zero for a disastrous controversy that surfaced when he didn't receive Abraham's inheritance. This created a historical division between the descendants of Ismael, pitting Islamists against the Jewish nation. We're all too familiar with this acrimony.

Abraham and Sarah, who were at one point impatient, later exercised their patience. Even though they scoffed at God's promise they could still have a child, they were patient and waited for His deliverance. When both Abraham and Sarah were around a hundred years old, they bore a son, Isaac. Patience paid off.

Jesus

We can't discuss patience in the Bible without focusing on our Lord Jesus. How many times did He show His patience with the disciples who were slow to understand His mission on earth? How patient was Christ after Peter denied Him three times? Then there's Jesus's patience when His good friend Lazarus was sick and dying. The Lord didn't run to his aid; He prayed and was patient. How many times did Jesus exhibit His patience when others didn't quite understand what He was trying to communicate? The lady at the well comes to mind, or when writing in the sand to determine the fate of an adulteress. He also showed patience and understanding with Thomas, who doubted His resurrection. Jesus was the ultimate example of human patience and someone we should pattern our lives.

God

Discussing the earlier examples of patience shows how strength of character, wisdom, and self-discipline flexes our patience muscles. But on a different level altogether is God's patience. How many opportunities has He given us, time after time, to redeem ourselves? Think of His patience with Adam and Eve; with Abel; Jonah; Noah; Sarah; Abraham; Moses; Joshua; and with Joseph, son of Isaac; and Job. And look at the patience He granted to Paul. In his early life, Paul terrorized the Jewish community, and God's patience eventually led Paul to see the light, literally. This man whom He granted such patience, went on to write much of the New Testament. Think of the patience God has had with us. Time after time we sin, yet God always forgives when we seek His mercy. God's patience is different. It's divine patience. Thanks be to God for His patience.

Now that we have such powerful examples of patience, let's use these as spiritual guideposts to help us navigate our course. Yield to the Holy Spirit; know the Spirit is there to help us with this weakness. Let us emulate Job and ask the Lord to give us discernment and strength to persevere. Be thankful for burdens, knowing they create new strengths as we fight through whatever difficulties confront us. Let us pause, and use the time to consider our responses before reacting. Invoke wisdom as James so eloquently wrote in James 1:19, "My dear brothers, take note of this: Everyone should be quick to listen, slow to speak and slow to become angry." Develop a way to respond to crisis situations by using the OPA. Finally, let us remember to pray to God for guidance. These disciplines cultivate character, help us grow dependent on God, and allow us to emulate Jesus Christ.

Dear heavenly Father, grant us patience. We are weak and need the Holy Spirit to give us strength to battle our everyday tribulations. In Your hands we place our lives. Amen.

CHAPTER 5
Pride Burns Brightly

OF ALL THE sinful natures, pride is the worst. Pride shows itself in many forms. Anything we do wrong while living on this spinning planet can usually be traced to some variation of spiritual pride. Such habits as arrogance, insensitivity, defensiveness, envy, self-absorption, overvaluing possessions, lack of forgiveness, and stubbornness are limbs of the tree that sprouts from the root of pride. Pride can be both an attitude and a behavior. Pride can be a mental state of mind, but it can also be the way we carry out our existence.

Spiritual pride should not be confused with its close relative, being proud. It's true the word "proud" is the past tense of someone exhibiting pride. But in our discussion, know that being proud isn't always a negative. Being proud of our wives, our children, or grandchildren is not spiritual pride. Being proud of one's accomplishments is okay too, as long as we acknowledge that we're operating with the gifts God bestowed upon us. Being proud and being humble are not mutually exclusive. We can certainly be humble when being proud.

What Pride Looks Like

God hates prideful exhibitions, mostly because it's sending the message to Him, "I don't need God. I'm doing fine on my own. Look at me and what I've accomplished." It shifts the confidence we should derive from God to self. Pride is the one sin that is most likely to keep us from crying out for God. Do any of these sound familiar?

- That guy cut me off. I'm gonna pass the car in front of me and box him in.
- I can do better than her; she was lucky.
- My home makes theirs look small.
- I'm so much smarter than she is.
- I'll never apologize to him; he doesn't deserve it.
- They cut in line in front of me.

- She sat where I wanted to; that irritates me.
- See how good I look in my new clothes.
- It's her turn to wash the dishes; I've done my turn.
- He never agrees with me.
- That person on the 1-800 line won't take time to fix my problem.
- I'm gonna get there first, just watch.
- I'm a Christian, and I feel sorry for them; they'll never make it to heaven.
- That waiter's not giving me the time of day.
- He doesn't know what he's talking about.
- I'll never speak to them again.
- He crossed the line this time; I can't trust him.
- She took the food I wanted.
- I'm the best-looking person here.
- Our team won; we made them look bad.
- They're neophytes in their faith; they don't know anything.
- I'll make them wait and finish when I'm good and ready.
- I'm not taking my car; it's their turn.
- They're gullible. I'll charge them more.
- He jumped in the elevator before me.
- I'm not gonna tell her; she'll have to figure it out on her own.
- He can find our house; I'm not gonna hold his hand.
- I'll get on the weight machine before he does.
- I know that scripture; they're wrong.

Sound familiar? You bet they do. We're all guilty, probably multiple times a day. Notice a common element in each sentence? How many times do we see the words "I," "I'll," "I'm," "our," "me," "my," and "mine"? Point of fact: All these examples include one of these self-obsessed words or it's implied. It seems many of us don't realize we're not the center of the universe. God is.

Why are some of the people we encounter so self-oriented? It's time for amateur psychiatry hour. As infants we are totally dependent on our parents, predominantly mothers at first. Our babies think, feed me, hold me, clean me, love me. It's all about "me". That's all these little people understand and it's how their brains are programmed from birth. It's an inherent focus on self. Following this premise, some kids grow into adolescence and teenage years prone to being coddled, given to, and over-provided for. Those receiving this over-provision and who receive more than they earn or deserve sometimes tend to develop selfishness. This is but one example how we raise children to turn out more prideful, to resent authority, and to feel more entitled than others. This cause and effect is certainly not true in all cases but could be a contributing factor to this kind of behavior. Regardless of the reason, it seems that we all suffer varying degrees of spiritual pride. So if it's inherent, how do we combat this unfavorable personality flaw?

Making Progress against Pride

The first step is awareness. Once we know what constitutes pride, we can observe ourselves in prideful acts. When words come out that don't pass the test of righteousness or humility, we should figuratively bite our tongues and regret what we said or did. Then we should put a sticky note on our minds to avoid these types of actions in the future.

James 4:6 says, "God opposes the proud but gives grace to the humble."

Fabienne Hartford, a writer and counselor for the Austin Stone Counseling Center in Austin, Texas, has a good understanding of pride: "Pride will kill you. Forever. Pride is the sin most likely to keep you from crying out for a Savior." She goes on to say, "Pride infects our eyesight, causing us to view ourselves through a lens that colors and distorts reality. Pride will paint even our ugliness in sin as beautiful and commendable." Later she says, "The comfortable moments when I pat myself on the back for how well I am doing are the moments that should alarm me the most."[38]

C. S. Lewis agrees: "According to Christian teachers, the essential vice, the utmost evil, is Pride. Unchastity, anger, greed, drunkenness, and all that, are mere flea bites in comparison."[39]

Jonathan Edwards was an American revivalist, preacher, philosopher, and Congregationalist theologian in the 1700s. In his essay *Undetected Spiritual Pride*, there are seven symptoms of pride.

1. Fault finding
2. A harsh spirit
3. Superficiality
4. Defensiveness
5. Presumption before God
6. Desperation for attention
7. Neglecting others

Number 5, Presumption, needs some explanation. He explains, "humility approaches God with humble assurance in Christ Jesus. If either the 'humble' or the 'assurance' are missing in that equation, our hearts very well might be infected with pride. Some of us have no shortage of boldness before God, but if we're not careful, we can forget that he is God."[40]

The more we dwell on these insights, the more it becomes obvious pride is the opposite of love. Domenic Marbaniang is a professor at the Central India Theological Seminary. He has an interesting perspective on pride. He takes words from 1 Corinthians 13:4–8 that define biblical love and applies an inverse slant telling us what pride represents juxtaposed to love.

Pride does not suffer long and is not kind;
Pride envies;
Pride parades itself,
Is puffed up;
Behaves rudely,
Seeks its own,
Is provoked (touchy and fretful),
Thinks evil (keeping record of wrong done to it);
Rejoices in iniquity, but does not rejoice in the truth;
Never bears anything,
Never believes anything,
Never hopes anything,
Never endures anything,
Pride always fails.[41]

Pridometer

We can begin to measure our daily activities on something we might call the pridometer. It would be interesting to see how many times we act humbly and don't lapse into the red zone, exceeding 2.5 on the meter. How often do we break through the humility zone and redline into the dreaded territory of pride? And if we do, how high does the needle register? It might be helpful for us to use the pridometer as a mental metaphor to help manage our efforts, thus improving our humility and reducing our pride.

PRIDOMETER

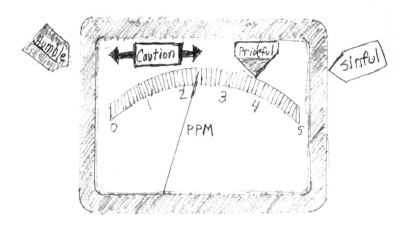

Jeremiah 9:23–24 reads, "Let not the wise man boast of his wisdom, or the strong man boast of his strength or the rich man boast of his riches, but let him who boasts boast about this: that he understands and knows me, that I am the Lord, who exercises kindness, justice and righteousness on earth, for in these I delight,' declares the Lord."

> Conceit is God's gift to little men. (Bruce Barton[42])

> The devil wipes his breech with poor folks' pride. (Ben Franklin[43])

> Remember, when the peacock struts his stuff he shows his backside to half the world. (Herve Wiener[44])

In concluding our discussion on pride, we should think before we speak or act and raise our awareness about the attitudes we're transmitting to others. The more mindful we are of our thoughts and actions, the more we can channel love as opposed to pride. Lastly, let's measure ourselves on the pridometer, and keep the darn needle in the refuge of humility.

Dear Lord, help us be more aware of our prideful natures. Give us strength to fight through situations that trigger pride. Assist us to overcome temptation and to be humble and in control. Amen.

CHAPTER 6
What's That I Hear?

AFTER ALL THE heavy thinking and poking around into the depths of our minds in the previous chapters, it behooves us to take a breath and enjoy something that doesn't tax the mental hardware. Following the Doobie Brothers' advice, let's "Listen to the Music." In an article written by Bob Kauflin on *Christianity.com*, he speaks about the importance of music to worship: "Music is a language of emotion in every culture of every age. It is capable of effecting us in profound and subtle ways. (like when Saul's spirit was calmed by David's harp)."[45] According to Mr. Kauflin, the Bible has over four hundred references to singing and fifty direct commands to sing.[46]

Music helps us enter into God's presence. It glorifies God, proclaiming who He is and our awe of Him. Music praises God and thanks Him for what He has done for us. Music helps us to worship our Lord, and surrender our lives to Him. It's a sacrifice of praise as a gift to God. The sounds help us relax and heal emotions. It teaches God's

Word and helps us learn Bible verses. Music is much like a celebration and in the case of the Bible's Song of Solomon, there's even love songs. With all this in mind, let's look at some inspirational songs that can help us worship God and unlock the emotional passion of our hearts.

Songs of Inspiration

One of my favorites is "Childhood Dreams" by Nelly Furtado. It has a reverence that's hard to capture in song, but she pulls it off. Not sure it was intended to be a spiritual song, but I treat it as such, because it moves me and is reminiscent of all the challenging times and bounties of life. The most striking quality of her song is the emotional vocals she expresses lyrically. When she talks about sliding on the rainbow of her childhood dreams and how happy she becomes when she's carried along, it touches me deeply.

Eva Cassidy was one of the most talented female vocalists to grace the airways in the twentieth century. Never heard of her? Take a minute to find her songs. She sings "People Get Ready," by Curtis Mayfield. The song is about being prepared to leave for heaven. It's poignant and stirring. Another of Cassidy's songs, "Over the Rainbow," written by Yip Harburg, made famous by Judy Garland, is the best version I've heard and brings a tear to my eye each time I listen. Unfortunately, at the zenith of her career, Eva passed away at age thirty-three from cancer. I lament losing her wonderful talent yet encouraged to know God has this angel singing in the heavens. Eva Cassidy's dreams really did come true.

"Be Thou My Vision," sung by Steve Ivey and Taryn Trexler, is a more traditional tune. It might sound familiar from hearing it in worship. It's included here since the lyrics are devout in their honor and praise of our Father God. What makes this tune special is the harmonization between Ivey and Trexler.

Recall the night a female vocalist was nearly laughed off the stage when she strolled in front of Simon Cowell and others on the TV show *Britain Has Talent*? More than likely it was because of her humble dress and plain appearance that led to the assumption she didn't belong on stage that night. The crowd and Simon were stunned into silence after Susan Boyle—the ordinary, middle-aged lady from Scotland—began her rendition of "I Dreamed a Dream." A must listen is her version of "Amazing Grace." The old spiritual tune brings back memories of what makes us appreciate our Lord and Savior sung by a woman handpicked by God, ordinary in ways and extraordinary in others.

While mentioning "Amazing Grace," there's another interpretation sung by Wintley Phipps, a native of Trinidad and Tobago. It gives the classic song a totally different feel with his booming baritone.

Another powerful and emotional song is "Show Me," sung by Audrey Assad. It captures the imagination with dramatically vivid lyrics. Assad sings about the end of her life and asks God to stay with her as she disappears. This piece has one of the most impassioned pleas to God I've heard.

When talking about inspirational music, we'd be remiss if we failed to mention some of today's celebrated artists, especially Hillsong United. The band's new-age worship music inspires, entertains, and praises God. The talent this group possesses is second to none, even compared to more popular secular acts. If you've never been to one of their live performances, it's a miracle unfolding in real time. It would be an unforgettable experience if a tour brings them to your town. Just a few of their many songs that warrant mentioning are "Broken Vessels," "So Will I," "Highlands", "Another In The Fire" and "Touch the Sky." Also check out NEEDTOBREATHE's, "More Time", Switchfoot's, "Dare You To Move", Cory Asbury's "Reckless Love" and Chris Tomlin's "Good Good Father".

For those into rock music, you should check out this one. Back in the seventies, when I was a teenager, a band called Pacific Gas &

Electric released a version of "Are You Ready?" on their album of the same name. It's an up-tempo, hard-driving, electric-kinetic tune that sheds light on how gospel songs were sung in Southern Baptist churches many years ago, albeit with electric instruments. Guitar solos? This song has one of the best of the era and carries with it a solid message.

"Music enables us to turn to the Lord in agreement with one another as we sing the same words and melodies, powerfully depicting the unity that is taking place. Music is used 'by God to draw us closer'—closer, he means, in the sense of drawing our gaze to the cross of Christ"; this is a quote from an unidentified author of a post on *The Hymnal Blog*.[47] This emphatically underlines the significance of worshipping through music.

Dear God, open our ears so we can go beyond merely hearing music. Teach us to listen and appreciate the subtleties so we can pay close attention to the message of Your love. Amen.

CHAPTER 7
The Vanishing Art of Forgiveness

Two Wrongs

SEVERAL YEARS AGO I spoke to a friend who handpicked a manager-trainee to take his place in preparation for pending retirement. At first the two got along famously. The trainee was thought to have a great future. They had the luxury of having a two-year training period to make a smooth transition. After a year, the trainee began having difficulty with his leadership and delegation skills. In a meeting with the regional director, the three discussed the need for the trainee to work on these competencies and to show improvement. The trainee was upset about being put on the spot. The trainee proceeded to blame my friend, (his manager), for circumventing his ability to be effective in those areas. He claimed that my friend, who was still training him, would interfere or disagree with his approach to handling certain situations, thus rendering him ineffective. Even though the regional director recognized the trainee's defensiveness for what it was, it stung my friend when his trainee left him in the lurch.

After the meeting, their relationship changed drastically. My friend harbored ill will and resentment for the way the trainee conducted himself toward what was considered to be a constructive session to encourage his effectiveness. The trainee's actions gnawed at my friend for months, which led to feelings of scorn and hatred toward the young apprentice. The last year of training was strained and tense. My friend discontinued providing guidance or direction, and pretty much just let him do his own thing. This situation haunted him day and night, and the more he fumed over what happened, the worse his disdain for the trainee became. After several exhaustive months, he grew fatigued from the mental horsepower devoted to the ordeal. It became apparent to my friend he was guilty of not forgiving the trainee for what he did. At first he had no desire to forgive him. Then it became obvious the failure to act in a godly manner was what had tormented him for the better part of a year. Finally, on his way to work one morning, he asked God to give him strength to forgive the trainee. Then he spoke aloud, "I forgive you, I forgive you, I forgive you." From the moment he pardoned the trainee, my friend put the issue away and seldom revisited the situation. Granted, my friend didn't forget the episode, but he didn't view it in the negative context as before. This act of forgiveness eased the tension, and the relationship improved toward the end of his tenure. My friend realized how grossly proud he was during those several months. Had he immediately forgiven the trainee, it would have saved him hours upon hours of grief and thoughts of hostility. He found out the hard way. Failure to forgive someone impairs the person harmed more than the person who committed the deed. He suffered because of his stubborn pride.

I tell this story so that others can be saved from making the same mistake. It's not worth it. It may seem hard to forgive someone, but it's much easier to forgive than have an unhealthy attitude germinate within our consciousness. We're only damaging ourselves by refusing to forgive. The other person goes about his or her happy life while we're muddled in misery. Consider this: If we're ill, we'd take the pill the doctor prescribed so we could get well. When it comes to forgiveness, the pill we should swallow is our pride. Forgive quickly, and let the evil escape without allowing it to pitch its tent in our psyche.

> Be kind and compassionate to one another, forgiving each other, just as in Christ God forgave you. (Ephesians 4:32)

God Can Forgive, So Why Can't We?

Embedded within the Lord's Prayer is how we agree to forgive those who trespass against us and we ask for forgiveness for our trespasses. The words are there for a reason. God gave up His most prized possession, Jesus. His Son was offered as a sacrifice to atone for our sins and to offer forgiveness. God is eager to forgive. He doesn't hold back. Forgiveness is available whenever we need it. All we have to do is ask for it humbly. We need to forgive in the same way and with the same degree that God forgives us for our sins.

> For if you forgive men when they sin against you, your heavenly Father will also forgive you. (Matthew 6:14)

The night before the crucifixion at the Last Supper, Jesus said, "This is my blood of the covenant, which is poured out for many for the forgiveness of sins" (Matthew 26:28). Every time we take communion, we should remember these words so forgiveness won't be so difficult to surrender. This way we can remove the chains torturing our minds, the chains of bitterness and resentment that can lead to anger and hate.

A True Act of Forgiveness

We've all heard unusual stories about forgiveness. There's one that's stuck with me for years. My friend and his family left church after service one Sunday morning to go home. He was in a van with his wife, daughter, and their foster child. As they were proceeding through a green light very close to home, they didn't see a car quickly approaching. The driver of the other vehicle was inexplicably flying down the Plano thoroughfare at over a hundred miles per hour in a forty mile zone. When the light turned red, the driver decided to blow through it. He saw my friend and his family's vehicle pull into the intersection, but it was too late for him to stop. All four members of the family were killed instantly upon impact. The other driver miraculously survived but was hospitalized with serious injuries.

The barrage of thoughts that might enter one's mind would understandably be contempt for the reckless driver. It was for me when first hearing about the tragedy. Yet a few days later, my friend's mother paid a visit to the hospital to see the survivor and perpetrator of the horrific traffic accident. She inquired as to his condition. During her visit, she forgave him for taking the life of her son and his family. In one instant their earthly existence came to an end. With her pardon, the mother instantly granted forgiveness to the other driver. She was a strong woman with great faith to do what she did. God gave her the ability to offer grace to the injured man. We should all be so forgiving, especially with the small stuff, and do so immediately.

> The weak can never forgive. Forgiveness is the attribute of the strong. (Mahatma Gandhi[48])

3 Steps of Forgiveness

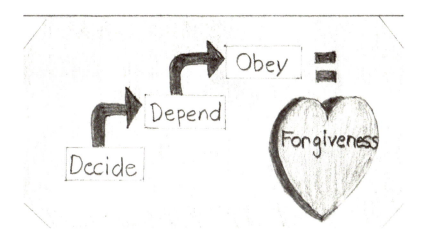

On her Web discussion *Everyday Answers,* Joyce Meyer makes some sense out of this conundrum in her article, "The Poison of Unforgiveness."[49] She spells out a simple three-step process that will take the yokes off our backs and free our souls for more important things. Here's a summary.

THREE STEPS TO FORGIVENESS

1. Decide: You will never forgive if you wait until you feel like it. Choose to obey God and steadfastly resist the devil in his attempts to poison you with bitter thoughts. Make a quality decision to forgive, and God will heal your wounded emotions in due time. (See Matthew 6:12–14.)
2. Depend: You cannot forgive without the power of the Holy Spirit. It's too hard to do on your own. If you are truly willing, God will enable you, but you must humble yourself and cry

out to Him for help. In John 20:22–23, Jesus breathed on the disciples and said, "Receive the Holy Spirit!" His next instruction was about forgiving people. Ask God to breathe the Holy Spirit on you, so you can forgive those who've hurt you.

3. Obey: The Word tells us several things we're to do concerning forgiving our enemies. For example, we are told to pray for our enemies and those who abuse us. Bless those who persecute you; bless and do not curse" (Romans 12:14).

GIFTS OF FORGIVENESS

Stephanie Caudle of *Huffpost.com* writes about the unimaginable forgiveness that was offered up after a catastrophic situation. Her article was based on a video of Black families involved in the Charleston, South Carolina, massacre that occurred on June 17, 2015. Dylann Roof was convicted for attacking the Emanuel African Methodist Episcopal Church, killing nine people. All those who lost their lives were studying the Bible. Caudle, who was inspired by the forgiveness of the families and other church members, came up with "10 Reasons You Should Forgive Those Who've Hurt You."[50]

1. It sets you free.
2. It helps you move forward with your life.
3. It begins your healing process.
4. It removes the anger and malice from your heart.
5. You're no longer giving someone else authority over your mind and heart.
6. You'll have peace of mind.
7. You have the power to forgive.
8. Forgiveness is the best revenge.
9. Forgiveness is one of life's greatest teachers.
10. Forgiveness helps us release the victim mentality.

As mentioned earlier, my friend's mother forgave the driver who killed her son and his family. The families and congregation of those murdered at the Emanuel African Methodist Episcopal Church forgave Dylann Roof. Shouldn't it be that much easier to forgive others for commonplace occurrences? As Joyce Meyer says, we can't do this on our own, but God's help and prayer will give us the strength to forgive. Let's remove the impediments from our minds and free ourselves to do more good in the world.

The *CliffNotes* version of what we've discussed:

- Immediately pray to God for strength to forgive.
- Forgive
- Go on about your life, and forget the past.

Lord give us the strength and wisdom to forgive others as You have forgiven us for our wrongdoings. Amen.

CHAPTER 8
Why Are Difficult People so Difficult?

———∽∽∽———

A NATURAL FOLLOW-UP TO forgiveness is how we go about navigating this topsy-turvy world with those who do not necessarily agree with us. There are plenty of difficult people out there who we'll have the displeasure of running into. But is it really a displeasure? This may not necessarily be the case. At some point we all face disagreements, arguments, conflicts, disparaging remarks, and provocations. How does God want us to handle these situations? Let's begin by pulling back the curtains on a seminal moment in the Good Book, found in Acts 15:36–40.

Paul and Barnabas

Here we find the story of a squabble that arose between the apostles Paul and Barnabas. Scripture says Paul suggested they go back to places where they had preached the Word of the Lord. Barnabas wanted to take John Mark along. Paul remembered when John Mark had deserted him and his group in Pamphylia, thus ending John Mark's work with the team. Because of this, Paul was adamant that John Mark not be allowed to travel with them. A sharp disagreement ensued, causing Paul and Barnabas to part ways. Barnabas and John Mark went on to Cyprus, and Paul chose Silas to go with him on his pilgrimage. What's interesting here is that even apostles like Paul and Barnabas, who were Christian leaders, devout, faithful men of God, could have disagreements. It's natural for our species to differ at times.

Urban wiseman saith: "Behold, if thou not knoweth the heart of a quarrelsome dude and he/she speaketh trash unto your countenance, get to knoweth thine enemy and quench the fire brought unto you."

What this imaginary, tongue and cheek oracle means, is find out all we can about the person to interpret his or her actions or feelings. What reasons might they have for their attitudes? People haul around heaps of thoughts, feelings, and memories, and at times it's unclear what they have in their outboxes. We have no way of knowing what's going on in their lives at that moment.

We should ask ourselves:

- Are they tired or not feeling well?
- Are they insecure mentally, physically, spiritually, or socially?
- Have life experiences taught them things we don't know or haven't experienced?
- Are they in a bad mood?
- Are they foreigners, yet to grasp the language?
- Have they been put in a situation that makes them uncomfortable?
- Do they lack social or behavioral skills?
- Are they impatient, in a hurry, or under pressure?

- Are they in a foul mood?
- Has something happened recently that affects their clear judgment?
- Have their egos been bruised?
- Have they been bullied or taken advantage of in the past?
- Are they competent or afflicted with a syndrome; mentally challenged?
- Are they on drugs or alcohol?

It's rational to ask questions about a difficult person before we react. Take a step back, and analyze what facts are known about the individual. Then try to understand their circumstances. Do we know the person's background? Have we given the person the benefit of the doubt rather than assuming something adversarial? We need to check our perception about the circumstance, and make sure we're not misunderstanding. Ask, what reasons might explain the person's behavior? Try to see the other person's point of view. Bounce ideas off a third person to see what he or she thinks about the person or the confrontation. Once we unveil what the person has going on between the ears—including experiences, health, phobias, recent incidents—then we can apply logic to determine how to react.

THOSE WHO DON'T LIKE US

I'm a pretty easygoing guy, and work hard to earn friendships. Most times I can get along with just about anyone. But every so often, I wander onto someone who flat out doesn't like me. I wonder if I remind them of someone who treated them poorly? Did I work in an industry they despise? Do they not like my jokes, hairstyle, clothes? Am I flippant, unintelligent, egotistical? More times than not, there's no clear cut answer, but I make every attempt to get along. The fact is there will always be someone who is confrontational, unfriendly, or just hard to get along with. We need to break down the barrier and find common ground to share with one other. If we want to grease the skids, pray to God for productive dialogue with that person. Ask to be given understanding of the mystery to their personality and the ability to offer friendship and assistance to their life journey. Pray for some sort of connection. Then with God's wind at our backs, we can challenge ourselves to break through the barricade, hop around the minefields, sneak under their veils of resistance, and commence to disarm their hostilities.

THE CHRISTIAN APPROACH TO CHALLENGING PERSONALITY TYPES

Individuals can generally be classified into certain personality profiles. After thoroughly cross-examining comments from psychologists and corporate training websites, added to my years of personal experience, I was able to piece together clusters of personalities classes. We all probably exhibit some of these traits, but obviously some show more than others. After each description, there's a simple approach to understanding each person's mannerisms and how best to behave in a Christian manner.

> *The Bully*: This is a person who tries to intimidate others. The bully can be harsh, abusive, pushy, or hostile. This attitude is often brought about by considerable insecurity. A good way to handle this person is not to challenge him or her. Let the person fire the initial volley, and allow the shrapnel to fall harmlessly around us. Once the bully sees we're not fazed by the bombardment, use kindness and a

genuine interest in his or her situation to disarm the person.

The Prima Donna: This individual is usually very well informed and appears to be an expert on the discussion or subject matter. Knowing facts and being confident with his or her knowledge gives the individual a feeling of superiority and allows the person to be the center of attention. When encountering this personality, it may be best to take a step back and listen. Ask pertinent questions, and rouse their intellects by showing genuine curiosity about their proficiency. Once we show an interest in and appreciation for what they have to say, it will provide an opening for us to enter their inner sanctums.

The Pessimist: This is a tough one. Once we know this person's type, treat the individual like a box of china dishes. This person is obviously in some sort of pain from past disappointments, family issues, recent tragedies, adversity, depression, or some other mental challenge. Be positive, and offer encouragement; avoid insulting them or sounding cheesy. Negative people tend to be drawn to those more positive so they can feed off the energy. Nourish gently, and try to bring them alongside to a more positive way of thinking.

The Aloof: Another difficult personality type. These individuals are hard to measure and know exactly where they're coming from or where they're headed. The aloof personality can be hard to engage because they may seem disinterested or indifferent. They don't offer personal information and may keep us at arm's length. It's obvious they're afraid to let others enter their realm. Respect the person's distance, and whittle away at the edges with bona fide interest in him or her as a person. Accept the challenge to become more familiar with what makes the aloof person tick. Poke around until finding a hot spot within the individual's catalogue of interests. Spend time exploring that area. Show unfeigned attention to their lives and what they're interested in, which can eventually break down the barriers. Take it slow. If they get wise to the tactics, they'll run for the hills.

The Passive/Aggressive (PA): A PA person doesn't feel comfortable confronting directly and will skirt around the issues, looking for ways to take shots when we're not looking. This doesn't necessarily mean they're being subversive or contemptuous; they're just not comfortable being direct. Take this person for what he or she is, and don't be ambushed by subtle barbs or surprises. They often use jokes or sarcasm to accomplish their missions. When dealing with a PA, try to redirect their approaches from the far-side aisle to the more comfortable center aisle, where genuine conversations can take place. Make them aware that we recognize when they're trying to be aggressive, and ask them politely to call a spade a spade. Once they realize we understand their approach, they'll be inclined to be more straightforward.

The Thwartist: I made up this word, so there's no need to check the dictionary. A thwartist is someone who likes to throw a wrench in something. They typically exhibit envy and suspicion toward those who they feel have it together. So in order to elevate themselves to higher levels or undercut those who appear more level-headed, they'll try to gum up the works. There are confidence issues with the thwartist, as there are with bullies, so they must be handled firmly and resolutely when they try to intrude. In a kind, Christian manner, disclose that we're aware of what they did and are curious why they chose that strategy. Once they know we're aware of their modi operandi, they might make corrections and respect our ability to diagnose attempts to derail the cars heading down the track.

The "It's My Pleasure" (IMP): This is someone who places a great value on being liked and is generally non-confrontational and apologetic. This is by far the nicest and most pleasant type of challenging individual in this classification system. They're easily damaged by complaints or criticism and have thin skin. They avoid skirmishes and would rather walk away from a fight than stand up for themselves. Once we know they are IMPs, treat gently, and make it obvious we're not a threat to their fragile natures. Mirror their attitudes, and once they sense we're of the same species, they will slowly become more bold, unafraid of any encroachments to their defenses.

The Bellyacher: This person needs no introduction. We all know the type—constantly complaining and never satisfied. They're a close relative of the pessimist, but they don't live in the same house. Nothing seems right or accurate to a bellyacher, and it becomes very hard to pass through the guarded psyche of someone who has such negativity. As we approach someone matching this description, counter each negative complaint with a positive rebuttal, showing a different way to perceive the situation. The more we pour positive salve onto their sour murmurs, the more likely they'll get the message, and it might just change their attitudes, even if only for a brief time.

The Missing The Point: The missing the point is an individual who gets lost in the minutiae of life. They can drown themselves in details and seek situations they can analyze and break into a million pieces. This is a person who will tell us how to build a clock after we ask them what time it is. Generally I find this personality type has an extremely high IQ. They get lost in explanations and seem to be exploring the insides of their minds for answers before replying. Much patience is demanded when talking to a missing the point. Carefully guide them back on track with gentle nudges and questions. Be cautious not to ask a series of questions while they're trying to formulate a response for the first of our queries. It could encumber the machinery, and the system may go down. We should respect their intellects but voice our interest to keeping discussions lively and moving forward.

In all these challenging personality classes a common thread is exposed: insecurity. We're all insecure to some degree, and it's up to us to discover what level of insecurity other people display and why. Once we know where they fall in these groupings, we can better understand their individualities. Then we can approach each one in a way that makes them comfortable and willing to engage us as a person. This technique will prove invaluable when trying to discuss our faith and belief in God. We shouldn't take a sledgehammer to a thumbtack. Use finesse, use love, use understanding and sensitivity. It will take us places no one else is allowed to enter.

If everyone liked us, and we got along and never disagreed, we would be lesser for it. Society forces us to adapt to different personality styles, disagreements, provocations, criticisms, and other forms of dissension we encounter. This forces us to learn, evolve, conform, modify, and transform. So it's important we don't linger too long in our comfort zone and avoid situations that are uncomfortable. To do so might inhibit our growth. We soon become educated on how to adapt, negotiate, placate, communicate, build rapport, earn and give respect, and when it's time to cut bait. Cut bait? This seems like such an uncharacteristic deviation to the objective. If we've prayed, asked God for His help, and tried everything we can to work with a person and they're still resistant to our offerings, it's time to move on. It may be the best option at that point to walk away or ignore—in a Christian manner.

Matthew 7:6 says, "Do not give dogs what is sacred; do not throw your pearls to pigs. If you do, they may trample them under their feet, and then turn and tear you to pieces." In the context of our discussion, I take this to mean- if we've given a good try to be friendly with someone or tried to share the good news of Christ and the individual refuses to come around, move on.

The Difficult Person Equation

Difficult Person × Understanding + Effort = Rapport

Dear heavenly Father, You made each of us distinct. Help us better understand our differences and give us the wherewithal to adapt to each person we meet so that we can improve Your kingdom for Your glory. Amen.

CHAPTER 9
Gossip

Don't

Dear Lord God, remove the gossip from our lips so that we can show You honor. Let us speak politely and avoid the temptation to disparage our fellow man. Amen.

CHAPTER 10

May I See Your ID, Please?

THIS EXCERPT FROM Charles Dickens's *A Tale of Two Cities* accurately describes the world's condition today:

> It was the best of times, it was the worst of times, it was the age of wisdom, it was the age of foolishness, it was the epoch of belief, it was the epoch of incredulity, it was the season of Light, it was the season of Darkness, it was the spring of hope, it was the winter of despair, we had everything before us, we had nothing before us, we were all going direct to Heaven, we were all going direct the other way …[51]

Dickens's quote inspires the question, Where are we exactly, that is, between the extremes? Along the same lines, the Dave Matthews Band released a song from their *Everyday* album in 2001 called "Space Between". The title of the song brings to mind the importance of the space between the beginning and ending chapters of our lives. When we look at the space between the two dates on a gravestone, this is where the story of that person's life dwells. The time between dates captures the essence of one's existence, but it seems like there should be more than just space. Do we merely live out our subsistence, or is there some greater plan for our lives? What is the purpose for each life to exist in God's world? "There is a time for everything, and a season for every activity under heaven: a time to be born and a time to die" (Ecclesiastes 3:1–2). Well then, who are we? Why are we here? What is our purpose? God gave each of us talents, abilities, and proficiencies in something. Mustn't we use these for the greater good? If not, why bother?

What Goes on in Between?
Grappling with Space in the Middle

Our identities are driven by our actions, religions, social positions, spouses, jobs, families, hobbies, appearances, and relationships, among other things. As the human race has evolved and become more knowledgeable and informed, it seems we're more inclined to focus on an introspective journey to determine our personal identities. People might say, "Who is the real me?" "I am the creator of my own destiny." "Who is the inner me?" "My life will be what I create it to be." "Who is the true me?" Okay, it is important to understand our personal identity, but the focus is trending more toward self-absorbing individuality, leaving God out of the discussion. Some of the areas we find ourselves exploring when attempting to discover our inner selves are egocentric exercises, such as:

- Relying on gut feelings
- Fulfilling personal desires
- Individualism
- Lack of restraint
- Self-legislation
- Instant gratification
- Excessive introspection
- Extravagant self-sufficiency
- Inordinate independence
- Unrestrained self-awareness
- Intolerance toward others

Some of these elements can be healthy in the right context. But we may be foregoing our Creator when we focus solely on our inner beings. As Scott Engle, PhD and the teaching pastor of St. Andrew United Methodist Church in Plano, Texas, says, "We must conform to the image of the one who created it, God."[52]

Paul writes in Colossians 3:9, "Do not lie to each other, since you have taken off your old self with its practices and have put on the new self, which is being renewed in knowledge in the image of its Creator."

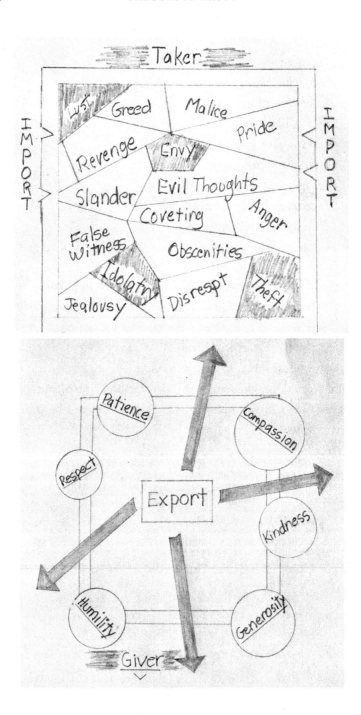

Are We a Giver or a Taker?

If we want to shed the self-serving, ego-driven habits and identify as a Christian, how do we emulate Christ throughout the day? Easier drawn than said. See image.

Box 1 is man's way; thinking of self. Notice all the elements within box 1—and there are a lot of them—are inwardly focused. We import these vices from external sources, feeding our appetites for self-fulfillment. Some prime examples are lust, greed, malice, pride, disrespect, anger, selfishness, gossip, and slander. We suck the elements out of life around us to feed our needs, which in turn become lives of idolatry. We idolize stuff we think will make us happy. In the first diagram, the more we feed our craving for internal needs, the more crowded it becomes with very little room to breathe. This also darkens the box as it becomes obscured with inward feelings, thoughts, and desires. These depict the internal characteristics of a taker.

Box 2 is God's way, thinking of others. God's way, shown in box 2, is quite different. Rather than sucking vices out of the world and jamming them inside our inner selves, God's model has us exporting goodness into the world, sending it *away* from our inner being. Such actions and traits like patience, generosity, humility, respect, kindness, obedience, and compassion are distributed to the outside world for the benefit of others. This outward-bound phenomenon opens the inner self and doesn't choke out the light of our soul. The space allows light to enter since the inner self is not congested. These are the internal characteristics of a giver.

The taker's box is dark, crowded, confused, jumbled, and disorganized. The giver's box is open, light, clean, clear, orderly, and fresh, all qualities of holiness. As Paul states in Colossians 3:12, "Therefore as God's chosen people, holy and dearly loved, clothe yourselves with compassion, kindness, humility, gentleness and patience." Clothed, I take this to mean what we wear on the outside, what we give away, what we're offering distinct from self. The similes about the qualities of light and dark make an emphatic point. Recall, "there is no such thing as darkness, it's just the absence of light"? In the case of the two diagrams, the absence of light in box 1 obscures any goodness. The light is always there; it's just blotted out. Lives aren't designed to have a cloud obscuring the soul. We need to rid ourselves of any cumulonimbus weather patterns, so we can see clear, bright, sunny skies.

Quoting Helen Keller again, "Keep your face to the sunshine and you cannot see a shadow."[53]

Damage Plan

By all appearances, the people who do their own thing apart from God seem to be living the good life. What shows on the outside, however, is never a true indication of what's going on inside. Eventually this lifestyle can end up causing damage internally and externally. Caught up in the wreckage are marriages, relationships, jobs, health, and respect. Most takers would admit—if they're being totally honest, they're lost, confused, lonely, and bitter. There's a hole in the souls, and they don't know how to fill it.

When we give ourselves to God and pray for His light to flood our inner spirits, we become more like what He designed us to be. Prayer, moral effort, and patience form a recipe for eternal life.

Are we a taker or a giver?

Dear God, teach us how to become a giver. Amen.

CHAPTER 11
One Step Removed from Our Comfort Zones

SOMETIMES OUR LIVES resemble a wagon wheel from days past, rolling along effortlessly in the groove carved out by the many wagons that preceded. If a wheel happens to hop out of the rut, damage could occur, or possibly cause confusion or uneasiness. The image that follows shows we're most cozy in our comfort zones. Does loving Christ mean we'll have to leave our comfort zones? Becoming a Christian is a radical decision. Think of it this way. Jesus gave up His existence so we can have eternal life. He accepted all our sins so that we can have a second chance. So the practical implication of living our lives for Jesus requires us to step outside of what feels comfortable. That's the least we can do for someone who died to save our souls.

Following Christ will certainly test the boundaries of our comfort. God calls on us to crawl out from the comfortable confines of our foxholes. Rather than shying away from the everyday bullets that spray around us, He desires for us to be aggressive, get up out of our safety zone and seek His will. This means helping the needy, assisting widows, orphans, the incarcerated, the mentally challenged, the aged, and those in poor health. He also asks us to teach the gospel. Find someone who is curious or in need of God, and share His story. Grow the kingdom. Spread the Word. Spend time in scripture; memorize verse. Keep a journal.

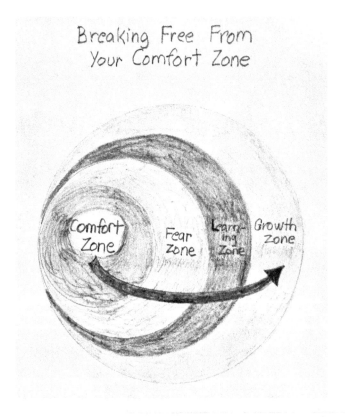

We must find a way to break out of these comfort zones. Doing so causes growth in our spiritual awareness and closeness to God. This growth doesn't come without some discomfort, but that's exactly what God wants, for us to be challenged and be uncomfortable at times.

Every time I hear the song "Do Something" by The Eagles, sung by Timothy Schmidt on their 2007 album, *Long Road Out of Eden,* I get inspired. The song reinforces God's desire for us to be part of His action plan. He wants us to *do something.* The song goes along the lines of, "Don't just sit around taking up space, you gotta do something." As I listen to this song, an image of God comes before me, and I get this visual of Him cheering me on as if I were running the last leg of a relay sprint. "Go, Greg, go. Come on, *do something*! You can do it!"

From scripture I think of all the folks that stepped out of their comfort zones. Moses argued with God against taking a leadership position to rescue the Jews enslaved in Egypt. He didn't think he could do it, but he stepped out in faith. *He did something.* Esther was completely out of her element when she was asked to attend King Ahasuerus's court to audition for the queen position. Not only was she a newcomer, but she was a Jew in the land of Persia, where royalty never married outside the noble family. *She did something.* Jonah refused God's call to go into Nineveh to preach against their wickedness. This was light-years removed from his comfort zone. He was so uncomfortable with the task that he ran away to hide and eluded God's presence. We all know the story that follows, where Jonah was swallowed by a "great fish" in what we might call today his "Come to Jesus moment." He finally heeded God's command, went to Nineveh, and proclaimed the Lord's message. What happened to the people there? They repented, the king of Nineveh declared a fast, and the entire city changed its evil ways. God had compassion and did not destroy the city after all. This all came about from one man's decision to step out and leave his comfort zone. *He did something.*

MISSION OPPORTUNITIES

I see many mission opportunities. Some are exciting and generate lots of enthusiasm to get involved. Others may not. At times I have to motivate myself to participate in less than inspiring activities. However, once I'm engaged in the mission, it seems there's always something new to learn, and I'm able to develop an awareness that might have been missing. And to be quite honest, mission opportunities almost always turn out better than expected. Breaking out of the comfort zone can open a new world to an otherwise unknowing individual. Think of all the people we'll meet!

Do Something!

Doing something outside our spheres of safety is counterintuitive because we're naturally inclined to seek comfort or safety; it's our very nature. The mortal inclination is to be self-reliant and take shelter in our comfortable environment. Abigail Brenner, MD, wrote some good thoughts in her article "5 Benefits of Stepping Outside Your Comfort Zone," from the *Psychology Today* website. Listed below are the five virtues of her discussion.[54]

1. Your "real life" is out there waiting for you.
2. Challenging yourself pushes you to dip into and utilize your personal store of untapped knowledge and resources.
3. Taking risks, regardless of their outcome, are growth experiences.
4. Don't settle for the mediocre just to avoid stepping out of your comfort zone, it's too big a price to pay.
5. Leaving your comfort zone ultimately helps you to deal with change—and making change in a much better way.

Gustavo Razzetti wrote about our comfort zone challenges in his *How to Leave Your Comfort Zone (for The Better)—Danger Is not the Opposite of Comfort.*[55]

This neutral state is both natural and human—our brain is lazy and leans toward the easiest path. We can continue living on autopilot or embrace discomfort to reap bigger rewards. Simply put: do you want just to live or to thrive.

Research has demonstrated that a state of relative comfort creates a consistent and steady performance. However, *relative anxiety*—a state where our stress level is higher than normal—can maximize your performance. Conversely, too much anxiety drops your productivity off.

The challenge is finding what Robert Yerkes and John Dodson called "Optimal Anxiety"—the sweet-spot between arousal and performance.

Here's what the Yerkes–Dodson Law Bell Curve depicts. It helps to see the concept in imagery.

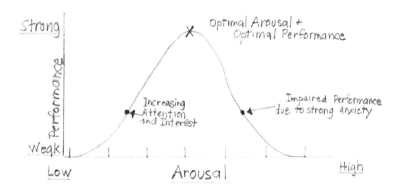

The Yerkes-Dodson Bell Curve

As we can see from the bell curve, when we expand our efforts, the stress level increases, and our performances are optimized. Conversely, if we don't push ourselves from the comfort zone, we remain weak, and arousal is low.[56] Once we break free from the comfort zone, we become outsiders, as seen when we inspect how the curve contracts at the top in comparison to the wider arc on the base of the x-axis. The term "outsider" is regarded as someone who departs from his or her existing cultural home for a new, unknown destination. So yes, Christians are outsiders. But we can bring a new perspective to others, new values, and unique ways of understanding. By becoming this outsider, we've turned into an insider with God. If we ever feel like we're walking upstream being a Christian, it's because we are. We're not following the crowd. Unfortunately, a number of our brothers and sisters are not in God's coalition. Here's some wisdom from those held in high regard. What do these deep thinkers say about following the crowd?

> It's better to walk alone than with a crowd going in the wrong direction. (Mahatma Gandhi[57])

> Those who follow the crowd usually get lost in it. (Rick Warren[58])

> Fortunately, some are born with spiritual immune systems that sooner or later give rejection to the illusory worldview grafted upon them from birth through social conditioning. They begin sensing that something is amiss and start looking for answers. Inner knowledge and anomalous outer experiences show them a side of reality others are oblivious to, and so begins their journey of awakening. Each step of the

journey is made by following their heart instead of following the crowd and by choosing knowledge over the veils of ignorance. (Henri Bergson[59])

THE WALL

Pink Floyd released an album in 1979 called *The Wall*. There's a song from that album called "Comfortably Numb," that describes the state we find ourselves if we never leave our comfort zone. Don't become comfortably numb. Get the first ticket out, and explore the regions beyond our horizon. Step out, and *do something*.

Dear Father God, help us to venture beyond the comfort zone into areas we are called to serve. Give us the courage to take that first step. Amen.

CHAPTER 12
Puzzle Paradox

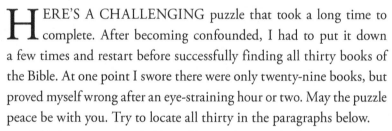

HERE'S A CHALLENGING puzzle that took a long time to complete. After becoming confounded, I had to put it down a few times and restart before successfully finding all thirty books of the Bible. At one point I swore there were only twenty-nine books, but proved myself wrong after an eye-straining hour or two. May the puzzle peace be with you. Try to locate all thirty in the paragraphs below.

This is a most remarkable and interesting puzzle. It was found on a desert island stuffed inside a hollow log by a man who was shipwrecked in the South Pacific. The puzzle location wasn't far from Honolulu. It kept him occupied for hours. He liked it so much he brought it back with him when he was rescued.

One friend from Texas worked on the puzzle while he fished from a johnboat. Another friend worked the puzzle while playing her banjo. Eleanor Johnson, a writer, was so intrigued by it she mentioned it in one of her books. A relative judges the job of solving this puzzle so complicated she brews a cup of tea to relax her nerves. Some books are pretty easy to spot. That's not fiction, it's a fact.

Some folks, however, will find themselves in a jam, especially because the book names, in most cases, are not capitalized. Truthfully, from answers we see, we're forced to admit it usually takes a priest, minister, or scholar to see some of them at the worst. Studies have shown that something in our genes is responsible for the difficulty we have in seeing the books in this paragraph. During a recent reunion, this puzzle was distributed at the Alpha Delta Phi booth and set a new sales record. The local rag, The Chronicle took a survey of over two hundred people, and they reported it was the most difficult they'd ever seen. As Daniel Athena humbly puts it, the books are all right there in plain view but hidden just the same. Those able to locate them all will probably hear lamentations from those who did not find them all.

A revelation that might assist you in your search is that books like Timothy and Samuel may occur without their numbers. Remember, too, that punctuation and spaces in the middle are completely normal.

A chipper attitude will help you compete pretty well against those who claim to know the answers. And don't get mad and make a quick exodus. There really are thirty books of the Bible lurking somewhere on this page, but they're waiting on you to be found.

CHAPTER 13

Ground Control to Father God, Can You Hear Us?

MANY PEOPLE WONDER, *How do we hear from God? Is He really out there? When we do hear from God, is it really Him?* Other questions surface. Do we hear voices, signs? Do lightning bolts strike around us? Just how does God communicate? These questions are much too heavy for a nobody like me to answer, so I went to some trusted sources to try and unravel the mystery. It made sense that if I collected enough information from those who are brighter, more educated, trained, and experienced, I could present some theories worth considering. Let's drink from the flow of this research and attempt to resolve the puzzle.

Many times we try to make communicating with God more mysterious or impossible than it is. We tend to overlook the obvious places for God's voice. Most experts agree that one of the most reliable ways to hear from God is through reading scripture.

The Bible

Everything we may hear or *think* we hear from God should agree with His written Word, the Bible. It's important to read scripture with an open mind and open heart with no preconceived notions. Furthermore, we shouldn't try to manipulate the verses in order to make them read like we want or uphold a position we're promoting. This approach is called eisegesis and goes against the grain of biblical truth. We know it's God speaking to us when it doesn't contradict scripture. A man I deeply respect and consider a mentor is Dr. John Tolson of The Tolson Ministries in Dallas, Texas. He often says, "the Bible is our manual of operation."[60] His point is: how can we operate the machinery without reading the operating instructions first?

The Bible instructs us. It speaks the Word of God through printed word passed on through generations. Scripture can provide answers we've been searching for, such as encouragement, guidance, or instruction. The pages between Genesis and Revelation were written by authors inspired by God. The Lord pushed the pen for those who originally wrote the verses. They were His scribes. So to hear from God, the most reliable, trusted way is listening to what God has to say on the pages of the Bible. Trust it, digest it, hear God speak.

Joyce Meyer always has valuable wisdom to impart. She says, "You can't hear from God if you don't know the Word."[61]

> All Scripture is God breathed and is useful for teaching, rebuking, correcting and training in righteousness. (2 Timothy 3:16)

Those We Trust

There are people in our lives who stand ready to answer questions and guide us along the path. They represent a second way for us to hear what God is saying. Our ministers, priests, members of our family, and friends are resources we should utilize. They can confirm the voice of God when we're uncertain of whether we've heard Him speak. Those who are mature in their faith can provide a sounding board for our ideas, questions, and concerns. The ability to communicate with each other about God enables us to grow spiritually. Discussing God with those we trust will reveal new thoughts and provide guidance. At St. Andrew we are very fortunate to have Dr. Scott Engle as our teaching pastor. Many of our congregants go to Scott with questions, and his sage advice and wisdom helps us find the right path to follow. The fellowship of those near to us also serves as an excellent way to interpret what we've read or have heard from God.

One of my good friends was married several years ago. His marriage developed problems based on the claim his wife heard messages from God. My friend came down with a sudden illness and was hospitalized. She visited him in the hospital and said she was being called by God to move out of state, hundreds of miles away. This meant leaving her husband in the hospital to recover while she made her way to follow God's calling. I had serious doubts this was God speaking to her. The Lord would never ask a wife to leave her husband in such a condition to pursue something that was mysterious and vague, especially like moving a great distance away. Sometimes we hear messages that are not from the Lord. It's essential that we stay on guard and not overreact to messages like this without confirming God as the source.

CIRCUMSTANTIAL CONFIRMATION

Christians, and even some non-Christians, ask God to give them signs. We hear, "God, please show us if the decision is correct." "God, let us know if we're headed in the right direction. Give me a sign." Many of us have probably asked for signs. It isn't uncommon to seek guidance from God to help us make the right move. If we look for indications, authorities suggest two things. First, we should not put God to the test. How is it possible for us as His subjects to test Him, the Creator of the universe? Second, come to God with a humble heart. Earnestly seek His wisdom, and be sincere when asking for His help and guidance. The Lord answers calls for those who believe in His kingdom.

We shouldn't overlook subtle signs that may float undetected under the radar. God can answer prayers in an inconspicuous or unconventional way, many times unexpectedly. Listen closely. Let's have our sonar tuned in to be receptive to any messages being received, even if ever so faint. It's the small voice that prompts us in our spirit. God wants to know we're listening.

Prayer

Prayer is the hotline to God's switchboard. If we want to converse with the Lord, we should pray. Prayer should be a conversation and not one-sided. We shouldn't tell the Lord what we need for Him to accomplish. We shouldn't be verbose, droning on and on. We should be direct and sincere, sharing our thoughts with Him and asking for instruction. While in prayer we need to be still and listen for His voice.

One day I hope to grow more accomplished at letting God reply to my prayers. It seems that when I begin praying, I tend to run through a list of all the people I'd like to help, and then I say, "Amen." That's not the way it's supposed to work. It's should be a two-way conversation. If we expect God to speak and we listen carefully, we'll have a better chance to hear from Him.

Another recommendation when praying to God is not to ask for stuff. It's not wise to ask God for a new car, for our contract to be accepted on the purchase of a new house, to get a promotion, or to get a raise. If we're looking for a positive response, consider adding the words, "If it is Your will," or, "God willing." Something like, "God, You know I'm up for a promotion, and this is something I've worked very hard to achieve. I would be humbled to receive the promotion if it is Your will." God seeks humility since the commodity is in short supply.

Holy Spirit

God's Holy Spirit is the advance man who delivers messages. The Spirit is one third of the triumvirate known as the Trinity. The Trinity is comprised of God, Jesus, and the Holy Spirit. One way to understand this concept is to imagine God as having two extensions rather than individual parts, "one God three persons." All three are in fact God. Each are tethered, working in union, not as detached entities. Imagine God as the CEO, Jesus as the director of sales and marketing, and the Holy Spirit as director of operations. God uses the Holy Spirit to speak to us, to deliver messages, to be a comforter, and to reside with us wherever we go.

Many leaders of Christian theology suggest that we recognize the Holy Spirit as a communication device. When we feel touched or being spoken to, it's God transmitting messages by means of the Holy Spirit. When trying to visualize the Trinity phenomenon, it helps to picture God's body with two arms, one Jesus, the other the Holy Spirit. Thus the description is often heard, "God in a body." Note that the Holy Spirit is considered a person, not a thing. Because of this we can speak to the Spirit and feel certain we're actually conversing with God.

Interpreting the Holy Spirit

Hearing voices and interpreting messages requires us to have full awareness. In my friend's case, his wife's message was from an unknown source and lacked discernment. A Christian, or anyone attempting to hear from God, should run the messages through a cerebral quality-control process. Does the message we're hearing:

- Bring peace?
- Inspire or improve us or others?
- Enlighten?
- Motivate us to better ourselves?
- Promote kindness as opposed to indifference?
- Lead us to do good?
- Agree with scripture?

If the message doesn't pass the litmus test of this spiritual filter, it's not from God.

The Conscience

When understanding the meaning of the word "conscience," most describe it as a knowledge of something we're going to do or say, have already done or said, or will do or say in the future. It's an internal by-product of a person's thinking mechanism no one can hear but us. It interrupts our thoughts, tells us whether we should or shouldn't do something, and critiques our actions. It's a warning device, a counselor, a cheerleader, and sometimes an, "I told you so," when we do something irrational.

The conscience is included in this chapter about communicating with God because it seems to interact with the Holy Spirit. Some believe the conscience is the Holy Spirit, but most experts agree the two work together, or in some cases oppose each other. We're all born with a conscience that has been nurtured for years, before we even understand the concept of God. By the time we come into God's sphere, past life lessons have been preprogramed as parts of our inner psyches. This being the case, internal controls are set to influence how our conscience will react to certain situations. Unfortunately, this doesn't mean our presets are always in accord with the Holy Spirit's guidance. There may be disagreement. In such cases the conscience will find ways to excuse the actions when they're sinful. Yet when we become a follower of Jesus Christ, the conscience is restored to be more in line with our faith. Ideally our conscience should become in union with the Spirit of God.

> When you became a Christian, a change began to occur in your conscience...He immediately set about to reprogram your conscience. (Charles Stanley, Pastor Emeritus, First Baptist Church, Atlanta[62])

As the conscience and the Holy Spirit come into alignment, our communication with God is enhanced, and the audible floodgates will open wide. Our conscience will be more proactive when presented with questionable options that don't parallel our faith, and it will point us in the right direction. We should affiliate our consciences with the truth. Walk side by side with the Holy Spirit, and watch all three bars on our spiritual phone light up.

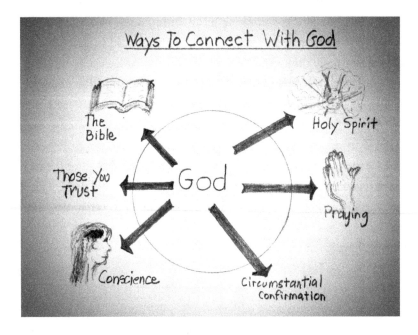

God speaks to us by His Word, sometimes by His Spirit, but even through our conscience. (Jack Wellman, Pastor, Mulvane Brethren Church, Mulvane, Kansas[63])

If all else fails and we still aren't able to hear from God in any of the ways described, we should check the dashboard to see why the engine light is on. Could any of these be the culprit?

- Our desire to hear from God is absent or slowly fading away.
- We lack humility.
- We don't feel worthy of God's time and attention.
- We have trouble letting go of the reins and allowing God to lead us where we need to go.
- We're not sincerely open to hearing His Word.
- We're skeptical that He will speak to us.
- Something—like sin, regret, or guilt—is blocking His communication.

If these occur, the best advice from the experts is to purge our minds first. Eliminate all the guilt, shame, regret, self-centeredness, and doubt. Once the runway is cleared, the conscience should accept the void. Then we should ask God to enter and fill our spirit.

God can speak to us; it's not an impossibility, and it's not difficult. The lines of communication are always in place. All we need to do is switch on our mental modems, and let the Lord begin the transmission. He'll do the rest.

> For God does speak—now one way, now another—though man may not perceive it. In a dream, in a vision of the night, when deep sleep falls on men as they slumber in their beds, he may speak in their ears

and terrify them with warnings, to turn man from wrongdoing and keep him from pride, to preserve his soul from the pit, his life from perishing by the sword. (Job 33:14–18)

Dear God, we want to hear Your voice. We need Your guidance. We come to You humbly asking for Your grace and peace. Help us open our minds. Enter and guide our paths. Amen.

CHAPTER 14
Dear God, Do You Want to Go Steady?

ALL JESTING ASIDE about going steady, how do we go about developing a relationship with God? This doesn't imply having a casual acquaintance like, "Yeah, I know who He is," or, "Yes, I've heard of Him." Rather it calls for a *real* relationship. It's sometimes hard to grasp, but God wants to be our friend. We can actually use the words "my friend." It doesn't have to be "my God," "my leader," or "my Savior." Simply call Him, "my friend." It does, however, beg the question, "How can the very author of the universe have any time or interest in being my friend, a nobody?" After all, each of us are but one random individual among the billions of people in our galaxy.

FRIENDSHIP

Most friendships we develop require active participation. We must be motivated and show the desire and willingness to spend time and put forth energy to cultivate a relationship. This doesn't happen on its own. A friendship is made of two individuals who seek an attachment and the desire to bond. The same holds true with creating a friendship with God. We must be willing to devote the time, energy, and desire to be His friend. True friendship is not passive. Our friendship with God, like any other, requires active participation.

Honesty

Most successful friendships display honesty as one of the cornerstones. If we aren't honest with one another, doubts can arise and trigger regret for not being straight. This creates a breach. True friendships don't have a breach; they're solid. Being honest is a quality that can be measured, and if it wavers, the poor judgment won't go undetected. Dishonesty is a high-maintenance activity. It takes a lot of effort to remember when we weren't truthful, safeguard a falsehood, or continually being cautious to protect a secret. The truth is so much easier to manage, with considerably less mental anguish.

God requires honesty. After all, He knows our heart anyway. He knows when we're not being forthright. It doesn't make sense to jeopardize our relationship with others and especially risk our kinship with God. Be truthful. Furthermore, the Lord doesn't seek predictable, pious cliches. We're better served to share our true sentiments, not what we feel obligated to say. Present God with our needs honestly and humbly; be candid and sincere. The avatar is honesty.

Trust

When a friendship is developed, the end product is trust. As in all relationships, we desire the ability to trust someone before we bare our souls. Friends want to be assured they won't get thrown under the bus or be called out unexpectedly. True friendship understands what's in the heart and strives to protect and honor a friend's interests. As our friend, God seeks trust to build a lasting relationship. He asks that we listen to His guidance, so He can lead us in the right direction. The Lord wants to share His love, mercy, kindness, gentleness, and honesty. To receive these gifts, we must trust the Lord. There's times we may find it difficult to see ourselves as a friend of God, like when Mike Myers and Dana Carvey said in *Wayne's World*, "We're not worthy." After all, He is the God of the universe, and we're just one of His many subjects. It becomes clear that this is a failure to trust. The operative word is "trust."

Imperfection

Be imperfect. No matter how well we perceive ourselves to have it all together, God knows our faults. He made us imperfect, like Adam and Eve. Think of David's lapse in having an affair with Bathsheba and being responsible for Uriah, her husband's death. Think of Peter's imperfections as a disciple, or the way Paul treated the Jews before his conversion. The phrase, "Nobody is perfect," applies to us all. We've all got damage; everyone has crosses to bear. It's incumbent upon us to be transparent with our imperfections and admit our faults to God. The Lord won't think any less of us if we sin or sustain a long absence. Imperfection is a key concept for us to remember. We're all imperfect. He's willing to forgive those who seek His absolution. Let's bring our baggage, and get aboard. But *do* get on the train.

Confrontation

This term has a negative implication. However, confronting someone may lead to understanding and appreciation of an individual's position.

God is not afraid of confrontation. He's not insulted when we confront Him with what's going on in our lives. Look at some biblical examples of how God was confronted. Abraham pushed back when the destruction of Sodom was near. He negotiated with God on the number of righteous people it would take to save the city. Moses complained that his fellow Jews wouldn't believe or listen to him. God told him how to overcome his fears, but then Moses complained about not being polished enough to speak. In Genesis, Jacob physically grappled with the very Creator of the universe. God accepts confrontation and wants to hear how we really feel. We should be frank and yes, be confrontational.

> I pour out my complaint before him; before him I tell my trouble. (Psalm 142:2)

Obedience

Obedience means everything to God. When we develop a friendship with God and communication takes place, He offers up wisdom and expects us to use it judiciously. We should trust in His wisdom, even if we don't quite understand how to proceed. The fact that we're obeying His mandates means something. We're being obedient. Obedience shows that we trust God and are willing to follow His directives. Furthermore, obedience can lead to intimacy with God. What could be more precious? Jesus said:

> As the Father has loved me, so have I loved you. Now remain in my love. If you obey my commands, you will remain in my love, just as I have obeyed my Father's commands and remain in his love. I have told you this so that my joy may be in you and that your joy may be complete. (John 15:9–11)

When we help the needy, share our resources, live honorable lives, encourage those who are down, offer kindness, forgiveness, and bring others to Christ, we're being obedient. God desires for us to do things for His kingdom, especially the little things. What may go unnoticed by some is quite obvious to God. As the prophet Samuel said, forget sacrifices, obey the Lord.

> But Samuel replied: "Does the Lord delight in burnt offerings and sacrifices as much as in obeying the voice of the Lord? To obey is better than sacrifice, and to heed is better than the fat of rams." (1 Samuel 15:22)

The relevant word presented here is "obedience."

Building a friendship with God should be paramount as we walk in faith. We should actively participate, be honest, trust each other, realize we have imperfections, and don't hesitate to confront God. We must be obedient. When we demonstrate these holy qualities, it develops friendship with our Father. The Lord's friendship means as much to Him as it does to us, and if we're willing to invest our lives to earn His intimacy, it will ensure eternal life.

Dear heavenly Lord, we want to be Your friend. We promise to dedicate our lives and make efforts to build a lasting, true friendship with You, our eternal Father. Amen.

CHAPTER 15
Ain't No Doubt

THE DOUBTER

IT'S A WONDER how a catchphrase coined nearly two thousand years ago still lingers in our vernacular. How many times have we heard the soundbite, "You're such a doubting Thomas"? The disciple Thomas was the only one of Jesus's closest followers who didn't quite believe He was resurrected. Granted, he didn't witness Jesus like the others when Christ initially visited the men and women. Thomas was the only person missing. When he reconnected with the others and heard the story of Jesus's appearance, the disciple disputed their claims. Thomas said he'd have to see Jesus's wounds before he believed. Jesus came back eight days later, and this time Mr. Doubtfire was present. Jesus offered His hands, showing the nail marks to give Thomas physical proof that He was the risen Christ: "Put your finger here; see my hands. Reach out your hand and put it into my side. Stop doubting and believe" (John 20:27).

Poor Thomas. he must have felt like an airhead. After he saw the wounds for himself, he said, "My Lord and my God!" (John 20:28).

Jesus proceeded with a message for all those present. The succinct message was meant for everyone, including us today. He said, "Because you have seen me, you have believed; blessed are those who have not seen and yet have believed" (John 20:29).

A humorous image comes to mind about Thomas. The vision on the mental big screen is when all the disciples are sitting around the heavenly table, talking, playing Texas Hold'em, fellowshipping, and discussing the bizarre politics on earth. After a time, Thomas says something that doesn't make sense, and his fellow disciples lay in to him unmercifully about it. This was followed by the disciples reminding him about his doubting incident two thousand years ago. They can't seem to quit ribbing him about his initial disbelief about Jesus's resurrection. They've been teasing him good-heartedly for centuries. The sequence continues, showing Thomas, leaning over amid all the laughter, turning red and covering his face for the millionth time. Then Jesus walks over and puts His hand on his shoulder and reminds Thomas that He loves him as much as everyone else. The other disciples encircle Thomas and give him a fraternal hug.

Could it be that Jesus purposely selected Thomas because of his doubting nature? Perhaps. Maybe Thomas's doubt was predestined so Jesus could prove a point after His resurrection. We won't know the answer to that part of the story until later.

A Daughter's Trust

Once there was a three-year-old girl perched on the ledge of a swimming pool. Her dad stood below in the water with arms outstretched, urging her to jump. The little girl had never jumped into the water before and was frightened at the risk she was facing. Her father urged her on, not once but multiple times, yet the toddler still wouldn't jump. She'd walk up to the ledge, look down, and then back off a few feet, refusing to make the leap. Finally she said, "I'm scared."

The father replied, "It's okay, honey. You can do it. Come on now, jump. I'm right here." She begins to whine, not quite convinced.

Then the young girl said, "But you might not catch me."

Dad said, "Don't be afraid. I'm right here. I won't move and won't let anything happen to you." Throughout this time, the father continued to show impressive patience and persistence. Finally, she gathered the courage and jumped. She landed in her father's arms, and you could hear the squeal of delight across the water. The crowd around the pool who had been watching, broke into applause after she finally made the leap. The three-year-old beamed from ear to ear with pride. The little girl wore out her dad the rest of the afternoon as she insisted on jumping off the ledge time and again. She shed her fear. The little girl had her doubts, just like Thomas. Finally she trusted her father and made the leap.

Faith in the Unseen

Has their ever been doubt that heaven is real or that beyond death there will really be eternal life? Ever wondered if there really is a God out there? As Christians, we don't tend to ponder these notions. It's through faith we believe them to be true. Admittedly I wonder about these things occasionally before quickly putting them out of my mind. What may help us put these thoughts aside is to remember Hebrews 11:1, which reads, "Now faith is being sure of what we hope for and certain of what we do not see."

If faith is being certain of what we don't see, doubt, by its nature, is the opposite. This poses the question if there would be any need for faith if doubt didn't exist. Doubt justifies the need for faith. In a world without doubt, there would be no need for God or faith. Could it be that God purposely implanted the seed of doubt in our DNA so it would necessitate calling upon faith? There's some rationale to this premise. The fact remains some folks inherit more doubt than others, as in the case of Sir Thomas.

We all have some measure of doubt. Can someone who has faith still have doubt? If I'm a good example, yes we can. The concepts are not mutually exclusive. Having a boatload of faith doesn't mean there can't be a hole in the hull where faith seeps out and doubt sneaks in occasionally. Our faith, even at its strongest, cannot totally eliminate doubt. We've probably all heard the saying, "Room for doubt". There will always be some presence of doubt, even if ever so slight. Since faith and doubt can't survive without the other, the interdependence causes the two to ebb and flow, exchanging real estate in the land banks of our minds. The goal should be to keep the doubt ebbing and the faith flowing.

It's up to us to determine what levels of doubt exist within our personal faith continuum. We need to keep close tabs on doubt, to keep from tilting the scale too far its direction. Let's look at Abraham's doubt valuation when God asked him to sacrifice his son Isaac. Abraham had no doubt. He believed. Abraham didn't think twice about killing his son in response to God's command. Abraham's faith was beyond comprehension, and his son was spared because of it.

Skydiving

Skydivers are an interesting breed. They soar into the stratosphere, jump from an airplane ten thousand feet above the earth, and at the last minute, pull the ripcord to release a parachute. The diver slices through the air at 120 miles per hour, is suspended below a chute made of thin nylon material, and hurtles toward earth. It's understandable how thorough these individuals must be in their preparations. The men and women study weather patterns and windspeed. Their equipment is checked and rechecked, and they always practice safety. The skydivers don't know for sure whether the equipment will work properly or if some freak accident might occur, but they don't doubt the outcome of a jump. If a person did, they wouldn't jump. These folks have faith that all will go well, and they'll live to do another jump. No doubts. All faith.

>   Our doubts are traitors, and make us lose the good we oft might win, by fearing to attempt (William Shakespeare[64]).

If an autopsy was performed on doubt, the forensic scientist would find:

>   Doubt is strongest during difficult times.

Doubt has battle scars from when it fights tooth and nail for fertile ground.

Doubt thrives when we have unreasonable expectations of God.

Doubt deceives us into thinking something dramatic needs to happen to rid ourselves of it.

Doubt is extinguished by truth.

When in Doubt, Don't

Wilton Herbert Hasty was a pilot and a captain in the US Army Air Force during World War II. He transported troops and supplies around the South Pacific, including New Guinea and Borneo. He spent many hours behind the yoke and often faced dangerous circumstances. From his many hours in the air, he learned something that was passed on to my siblings and me. It's a simple rule of thumb he taught me when I was learning to drive. My dad sat in the passenger seat and patiently coached me as I drove the streets of Dallas. I was only fourteen at the time and had no business being behind the wheel. But my father wanted me to learn how to drive at an early age, so I could log as much time as possible on the streets before getting my license. We were at an intersection in Oak Cliff, and I was idling at a stop sign. A car was coming to my left, and it was just far enough away for me to consider pulling out, but it was close enough to make me think twice. I quickly glanced over at Dad, and all he said was, "When in doubt, don't." This sage advice saved me from many situations that might have turned out for the worse. As it applies to our faith, if there's any doubt, don't. That is, don't entertain doubt; let it disappear in favor of our belief in God.

Richard P. Feynman, an American theoretical physicist says, "Religion is a culture of faith, science is a culture of doubt."[65]

Ever come across this short piece of wisdom? "Love is weakest when there's too much doubt." How can we be expected to love if there's constant doubt? If doubt overrides our abilities to love, where does that leave us with the mandate to love God, love neighbor? Faith in God, albeit similar to that of skydivers and toddlers, is much more significant and carries with it considerable eternal consequences. There's no way of knowing for sure what will be on the other side of our decision, but faith makes us jump.

Dear Father, help us to manage our doubts and not be afraid to jump. Amen.

CHAPTER 16

Give It Up; It's Not Ours Anyway

"**GIVE**" IS A short, four-letter word that carries a wallop. It generates a powerful payload. It's not passive; it's an action verb that calls for the performance of a physical act. To give is to transfer something of value to another person, thing, or purpose. It might be one of the most impactful words in our language. Give can also be used in the negative, like giving someone a black eye. The meaning we use here is the giving of ourselves for the good. Giving is contributing something of value that we own to others who have a need.

Giving Is Good

Why is giving a good thing? Let's unpack generosity to find out. Susan Bloom writes a poignant article for *Jersey's Best Magazine*. She reports that the act of giving, "can lower blood pressure, combat loneliness and depression, reduce chronic pain and stress, all of which can help boost the individual's immune system, fight off disease and promote longer life."[66] Wow! That's a basketful of positives for subtracting things of value from our possessions. The mere act of giving can do all this? Yes, and more. Ms. Bloom goes on to say, "A recent five-year study from the Science of Generosity Initiative at the University of Notre Dame examined 2,000 Americans and found that those who described themselves as 'very happy' volunteered at least 5.8 hours per month."

If giving does all these great things physically, how does it affect us psychologically? Ms. Bloom continues, "According to *Psychology Today*, the act of giving to others may increase the brain's levels of dopamine, a neurotransmitter involved in motivation and reward, resulting in a virtual 'helper's high.'" And, "Studies show that volunteering can help boost one's confidence, self-esteem and sense of purpose/meaning in life."

How about spirituality? How does this coalesce with giving? Juan Riestra, MD, and chief of psychiatry at St. Joseph's Wayne Medical Center, says in Ms. Bloom's article, "Studies show that people who hold some kind of spiritual belief that emphasizes goodness, love, kindness and sharing with others feel happier and live more fulfilled, healthier and longer lives.'"[67]

Since generosity contributes so many good things to us physically, mentally, and spiritually, why don't we do more of it? To better understand the phenomenon of generosity, let's look at the contrasting side of giving, its antithesis, *selfishness*. Selfishness boils down to the lack of regard for others and more interest in one's personal profits or pleasure. Selfishness is not a good quality.

Selfishness

Why is it that people are selfish? Remember the words in chapter 5 about growing up and being over-provided for? In our current day vernacular, we would use the term "spoiled." This individual can be prone to exhibit selfishness. It could be unintentional or subconscious. The act of being selfish might be an inherent self-preservation trait or a defense mechanism wired into the hardware at an early age. Selfishness is said to protect or achieve one's self-interest, and usually demands more attention to engineer or safeguard those self-interests. This characteristic might also indicate innate fear or resentment whereby giving may threaten their wants and needs.

Rewind a moment to givers and takers. Recall that takers seize the good from around us and congest the inner self with wants and needs. This is the taker. We know how detrimental it can be to plunder all the good in the world only to trap it inside. "What good will it be for a man if he gains the whole world, yet forfeits his soul?" (Matthew 16:26). Alternatively, a giver transplants goodness to others with hopes of nourishing growth.

Here's a few reasons why people give.

> "It makes me happy."
> "Giving helps others."
> "It reflects the character of God."
> "My giving seems to influence others to give."
> "Giving something to others teaches me humility."
> "It makes me feel better about myself."
> "I'm making a difference."
> "It's easy once you develop the habit."
> "I'm following God's will."

Throughout scripture we see God continually giving to His followers. The ultimate gift was that of His Son, Jesus Christ. What better gift could be given than Jesus and His ability to forgive our sins?

> No one is useless in this world who lightens the burdens of another. (Charles Dickens[68])

God, however, wants us to give willingly. If we're sulking or complaining about giving, we need to stop and examine our feelings. For something to be a true gift we need to give freely and sincerely.

> Give generously to him and do so without a grudging heart; then because of this the Lord your God will bless you in all your work and in everything you put your hand to. (Deuteronomy 15:10)

> Each man should give what he has decided in his heart to give, not reluctantly or under compulsion, for God loves a cheerful giver. (2 Corinthians 9:7)

As cheerful givers, we can enjoy many benefits. According to authorities we'll live longer, be happier, have less stress, feel better, make others happy, assist our fellow humans, and be difference makers. An important ancillary benefit is that it serves as an example for others. Notice the ripple effect as people observe what we're doing. In Deuteronomy, God says He will bless us in all our work and everything to which we put our hands. Our prayer should be to soften the hearts of takers and enlighten each one so they can begin reaping the rewards the Lord bestows on givers.

When It's Okay to Be a Taker

Let's turn things around. What if we're the receiver of a gift? Apart from being a cheerful giver, we should strive to be a gracious recipient as well. We often instinctively flash our "pride card" when offered help or assistance. We turn down good-faith offerings. There are times when we may not need the gift or don't want to appear dependent. It's common for us to feel uneasy, embarrassed, or even offended. As the recipient of a gift of generosity, we should be conscious of not only our own emotions but the giver's feelings as well. Readily accepting a gift from someone makes that person feel good. When we accept the person's benevolence, the giver is immersed in the feel-good hormone, dopamine.[69] Accepting a gift creates a bond. Alternatively, if a gift is refused, it causes a breach.

There's a friend to whom I've made numerous offers, and I consistently get the same answer: "No, don't do that. I don't need it." He seems to be appreciative, but if others are like me, I'm disappointed and feel uncomfortable getting turned down. It's like offering a handshake to someone who turns and walks away. I don't make these gestures to my friend any more because I know what the answer will be. This is not God's design. Don't steal someone's joy by refusing a gift. If we have it in our heart to help someone feel good, be a gracious recipient. Take them up on the offer; it will help them build self-worth, reinforce their generosity, and strengthen the relationship. It might even help us out in the process. It's a win-win.

Responsible Giving

Our focus now turns to responsible giving. This is what we can afford to give without negatively impacting our financial resources. What good does it do to give more than we're able, only to find out later we have nothing to give? We should manage our affairs such that we can be continual and consistent givers to God and His kingdom. Lest we forget the parable of talents, Matthew 25:14–30. A man goes on a journey and gives his servants money for safekeeping while he's gone. One servant invested wisely and generated a good return. He was given high praise on his master's return and was rewarded with more money and responsibility. Another servant was afraid to lose the money he was entrusted, so he hid it and didn't do anything constructive with what he was given. He had no return and was met with the angst of his master. This servant's money was taken away and given to the first servant. The message quoted from Matthew is meant to help the Lord's followers understand that we should deploy what He's provided. Not hide it away and be afraid to use what was given to us. The first man in the parable created more value since he was a good steward of his funds. He showed the upmost responsibility for what he was given. The other man did nothing and gained nothing, thus, he had nothing to give.

There's no prohibition to being wealthy in God's kingdom. What He does say is to be generous with what we've been given. Simple logic indicates the more we accumulate, the more we should give. He wants us to be responsible, so we can be a long-term giver to others and not become a taker. "From everyone who has been given much, much will be demanded" (Luke 12:48).

Giving to the Church

There are a number of places to invest our donations, such as global missions, local charities, homeless shelters, food banks, or helping the elderly and disabled. There's no end to the ways we can contribute. A good practice is to support causes that have low overhead so funds can go directly to the cause. Many times our contributions go to pay the salary of staff members of a nonprofit, instead of the needy. Personally, I prefer to see my gifts received by those in need. The one major exception to this line of thinking is giving to the church. As is the case with our church, and it is a big church, there are many expenses involved in keeping operations running smoothly. A church serves so many purposes and is the lifeblood of our community. It provides worship, grief support, missions, Bible studies, music, children and youth programs, men's and women's groups, and so much more. Along with funding these programs, there are the basic needs of the church, which require significant financial support. These are sometimes taken for granted. Essentials such as minister and staff compensation and benefits, mortgage or loan payments, utilities, insurance, building maintenance, custodial services, communications, and technology are foundational expenses of the church. There's so much that goes on behind the scenes. We should welcome hearing about capital campaigns and church budgets. This is all necessary to keep the pumping heart of our faith in good working order. As Leviticus 27:30 instructs, give things of value as a tithe. We should honor this command to keep our churches relevant.

Summing it up:

> Be generous and feel good.
> Be of help to others however we can.
> Be a cheerful giver.
> Be a good recipient.
> Be a responsible donor.

> We make a living by what we get, we make a life by what we give. (Anonymous[70])

> The best things to do with the best things in life is to give them away. (Dorothy Day, author, journalist, and social activist[71])

> To get the full value of joy you must have someone to divide it with. (Mark Twain[72])

Dear God, help us to be a cheerful giver and receiver. Let us be responsible with our gifts and show generosity to those in need. Amen.

CHAPTER 17

Heavens to Murgatroyd

THE TITLE OF this chapter was popularized in the 1960s by *The Yogi Bear Show*. The idiom was heard time and again on the cartoon from Snagglepuss, one of the characters, who would exclaim, "Heavens to Murgatroyd." It was his way of expressing bewilderment. Snagglepuss, heaven can be bewildering to us too!

AFTERLIFE

When did the idea of an afterlife arise? Studying ancient Egyptian rituals, these people were ardent believers in life after death. The tombs of the pharaohs were constructed to preserve rulers in preparation for immortality. As this relates to us, it poses a question: Is there something more after death, or is our demise a hard-stop? Do our bodies cease to function, and we drift through a no-return zone absent any spark of life remaining? It's frightening to fathom how our lives can be extinguished, leaving hardly a trace that we ever existed. Afterwards, where do our souls or psychic beings go? Is it complete nothingness, and if so, what constitutes nothingness? This lack of information added to speculation is what unnerves us about our mortality. It's the great unknown.

Doubt was discussed earlier, and it's a good time to reintroduce faith as the fail-safe for such moments of hesitation. Recall how faith is the assurance of things hoped for and the belief in things that cannot be seen. It's our faith that takes us beyond the scientific probabilities and theories that fall short of God's hierarchical realm. Mortality is one of those things that can't be explained with any absolutes. Therefore, through faith we rely on the words expressed in the Bible, assuring us of resurrection and eternal life. Trusting these words is essential. As Christians, we choose to believe there is a heaven, and if considered worthy, we will one day be there with God. So what's heaven like?

Apart from the excerpts found in the Bible, no mortal has ever seen the mystical place called heaven and later be able to speak about it. Therefore, no one can say with any certainty what it's like or if it truly exists. Those with faith, however, believe there is a heaven although it can't be described in any meaningful detail. Try as we might, there's no way to explain it with any certainty. The only clues we have are a few bits and pieces we find in the Bible. Before venturing into specifics, perhaps we should ponder whether God would really want us to be concerned with the logistics of our final resting places. Is it important? Then again, He might be glad we're curious, so we can be comforted with where we'll live for the duration.

The verses from the Bible that reference heaven have been consolidated here and presented in narrative form to provide a glimpse into what heaven might be like.

A Glimpse of Heaven

Heaven is a place; it is a city with walls. It will have streets of pure gold. It is a virtual paradise built for worship and a place of tranquility. It has pearl gates and a river yielding fruit on either side. The kingdom is adorned with precious gemstones. Heaven will have mansions where we dwell. The tree of life will be in heaven, shared by all nations and people who worship Jesus. Heaven will be filled with peace, joy, and praise. Heaven will have many rooms, and a place will be prepared for each of us when we arrive to join Jesus in His father's house. There will be no day or night, but the whole city will be lighted by the glory of God. It will be like a wedding reception, and we'll be able to feast with all people. Heaven is void of hunger or thirst. There will be countless nations, tribes, people, and tongues, all wearing white robes.

Taking these somewhat elaborate descriptions, let's overlay with what religious authorities have concluded about heaven from scriptural inferences. No matter a person's credentials, we must realize these are only speculations and assumptions. Some could be true. Who can say?

Heaven is a real place where God is surrounded by a heavenly court, a throne, and heavenly beings. Community is vital, thus engendering peace, love, and kindness. It is God's dwelling place and a kingdom set apart from the earthly realm but parallel in terms of the Lord's inclusive dominion. Heaven will be filled with light. God will dwell there, and He'll be able to communicate with us. Heaven does not exist outside our universe, thus allowing Christians who pass away to enter into the presence of Christ immediately. There will be angels among those in heaven, along with our loved ones. Nothing bad will ever happen. There will be no fear, pain, mourning, or crying. There won't be a church because God and Jesus *are* the church.

In heaven we will not need rest and will never be bored or exhausted. We'll worship without distraction and continue to learn indefinitely. We'll know every person; all will be considered loved ones, and there are no strangers. We will be the same people in heaven as we are on earth, minus our imperfections, absent of sin, which will be removed.

What's in the Suitcase?

I found this story written by Dial Hope on her website. It's about, "[A] man who wanted to take his money with him beyond the grave."

> One evening, when he was thinking about death, he prayed fervently about this. An angel appeared to

him and said, "Sorry, you can't take all your wealth with you after death, but the Lord will allow you to take one suitcase. Fill it with whatever you wish." Overjoyed the man got the largest suitcase he could find and filled it with pure gold bars. Soon afterward, he died and showed up at the gates of heaven.

St. Peter, seeing the suitcase, said, "Hold on, you can't bring that in here with you." The man explained how God had given him special permission. St. Peter checked it out with the angel Gabriel and the story was verified. "Okay," said St. Peter, "You can bring the suitcase in with you, but first I must check its contents." He opened the suitcase to see what worldly items this man had considered too precious to leave behind. "I don't believe it!" said St. Peter. "You brought pavement?"[73]

A humorous account that emphasizes how things we value on earth are worth little in heaven. And how magnificent heaven must be if gold bars line the road.

How Do We Get There?

Now that we have a somewhat nebulous image of heaven, clear only in the expanse of our imaginations, it leaves us with this question: How does one get to heaven? Similar to understanding heaven itself, no one knows exactly how we gain admittance to the Promised Land. There's some obvious assumptions about who *won't* get into heaven, but what are the chances of making it to paradise? Recall the thief on the cross next to Jesus. It didn't matter how sinful he was leading up to the crucifixion where he hung alongside Christ. After he showed his faith, Jesus forgave his sins and promised he would be with Him in paradise that day.

Let's lean on scripture for insight. In Matthew 7:21, Jesus answers the question: "Not everyone who says to me, 'Lord, Lord,' will enter the kingdom of heaven, but only he who does the will of my Father who is in heaven."

The "will" Jesus points to God's Ten Commandments. These ten laws establish a baseline of perfection. It requires flawlessness to enter heaven. God created us imperfect, so He knows it's not feasible to expect perfection. That's why He sent His Son, Jesus. God sacrificed His Son on the cross to forgive us for our sins. What this means for our chances to enter heaven is that we don't have to be perfect to enter. But we must be righteous and ask forgiveness for our imperfections and sins. If we're sincere and seek sanctification—the act of becoming holy—for our past missteps, Jesus will clear the way for us to enter heaven. Think of Jesus as our proxy. Jesus is the spokesperson who lobbies God on our behalf.

THOSE WHO DON'T KNOW JESUS

What about those who don't know that Jesus exists or are not familiar with God's commandments? Since some haven't had the opportunity to learn and follow God's commands, can they go to heaven? There's mixed reviews on the matter. American theologian R. C. Sproul says, "God never punishes people for rejecting Jesus if they've never heard of Jesus."[74] Robert Velarde, former editor of *Focus on the Family*, says, "We know that God will deal fairly with those who have not received a direct presentation of the gospel, just as He will deal fairly with those who have."[75] Both go on to provide contrasting perspectives about how a person's admission into heaven is not guaranteed, even if he or she isn't aware of Jesus or scripture. We can't be certain because no one knows for sure; it's pure conjecture. The basic theme of experts who show extensive wisdom on the subject is that every person should know there's a god, even if they're oblivious to Jesus and the gospel. The rationale is if a person doesn't know God exists, he or she must believe in some other higher being. So if the man or woman is not aware of Jesus and God, he or she must have a set of moral values that will be judged by God.

Clear as muddy water, I know. This is something we'll need to ask the Ultimate Authority once we're admitted to paradise.

When questioned, most people think they'll go to heaven. We may hear, "I hope so," "I think so," or, "I've got as good a chance as anyone." All these statements indicate an element of doubt, and from earlier discussions, we know what doubt means. There shouldn't be any doubt as to whether we're going to heaven. We can eliminate the doubt by exchanging it for faith.

A Losing Wager

For those who don't believe in God, it's hard to comprehend the rationale for the risk they're facing. The nonbeliever is wagering there is no God or heaven. They're staking virtually everything on this being true. It goes beyond betting money, investments, a home, or even their lives. They're gambling *eternal existence*. Think of the significance of this speculation. Why would anyone want to risk a roll of the dice, with such monumental consequences hanging in the balance?

For those who do believe in God, conduct themselves righteously, and ask for forgiveness of sins, they'll enjoy eternal life in heaven. There's no gamble. There's no downside; Jesus promises this. We should eliminate the guesswork and secure a guarantor for our eternal life, Jesus Christ.

There's a few things most Christians are in agreement. Those who are wicked and beyond reform will not be going to heaven. Even worse, individuals who renounce God, blaspheme, and deny His existence will accompany the wicked to the alternate destination. This is where they will remain for eternity. We hold out hope that those who reside in this community of darkness will eventually see the light, ask for forgiveness, and seek God's grace. "Helping people get into Heaven is the greatest act of mercy you can do for them" (Rick Warren[76]).

Dear God, please guide us to heaven. We strive to follow Your commands. Forgive us for our shortcomings so that we may be allowed to spend eternity with You. Amen.

CHAPTER 18
Calling All Angels

ONCE UPON A time, Almighty God was going about His day creating solar systems, galaxies, and tidying up the universe. The work was piling up, and He couldn't address everything that needed His attention. He considered working more hours or picking up the pace to accomplish more but decided neither was an attractive option. There was so much to do. Finally, God decided that He needed to whittle down His to-do list and start practicing delegation skills. Once the Lord formulated His plan, He created some assistants to do His legwork. God sculpted images of spiritual beings, so He could begin delegating chores. God knew the Greek word *anglos*, which was a beautiful, descriptive term that would affirm the new beings He created. Soon the Lord's designs were complete, and He assigned a name to His deputies. God called His subordinates, archangels, translated from Greek meaning "chief angels."

The Lord gave angels many skills to carry out their tasks and instilled emotions within their heavenly spirits. These skills would enable them to use their abilities to execute God's plans. They would be wise and intelligent. Angels were able to travel through time and distance with little effort and could work anywhere within the universe God presided. Each of the archangels were asked to sign a document with several prerequisites. He brought three archangels into His heavenly office, and each signed an agreement to glorify only God. These heavenly bodies pledged their undying faith to their Father, with the understanding they would not be figures of worship themselves. As part of the arrangement, the angels were given names, wills of their own, and supernatural abilities, along with assurances from God that they would assume the roles of heavenly intermediaries. These new positions would interface with the new creation He was contemplating. God's plan was to fashion a place for individuals made in His image to live a temporary life on earth. He would oversee the beings' creation and monitor their lives during their existence. The Lord would guide, advise, and instruct the human souls on the correct path to everlasting life.

Each of the archangels turned in their paperwork, and God collected the signed documents. One angel stood out; his name was Michael. Impressed, God asked him to be the team coordinator. He would work with the other archangels to organize a company of "soldier" angels to assist with the new world He was creating. God proceeded to bring into existence an abundance of these angels, too numerous to count. The archangels had a difficult assignment but undertook their God-given task to organize the new team in preparation for the big creation He planned.

There were long lines of angels in the queue who were likewise required to sign statements subjecting themselves to God's master plan. Slowly the archangels signed up the new recruits, one by one, until the lines were gone. God sat up late reviewing all the completed agreements, verifying each angel had signed His document. To an angel, they had all signed and agreed to the terms except for one. God inspected the single unsigned accord. The name at the top of the contract was Lucifer.

Lucifer AKA Satan

God brought Lucifer into His heavenly office and asked him why he didn't agree to the terms. Lucifer was argumentative and disorderly. He refused to honor God even though the Almighty was Lucifer's maker. God sent Lucifer away in disgrace, and the disgruntled angel swore he would do everything in his power to derail God's plan for the new world. The Lord had His hand on the destruct button as Lucifer turned to leave and had momentary thoughts of eliminating the disobedient angel. But in His ultimate wisdom, God let Lucifer leave unharmed. Later Lucifer was able to persuade one third of the angels to renege on their contracts to accompany him on his diabolic missions. His minions became known as demons.

With Lucifer and his underlings lurking in the depths of His new creation, God knew it would challenge the new living creatures to make good decisions. They would either choose to be righteous and follow Him, their Creator, or be led astray to the darkness by the maverick angel named Lucifer. *That's perfect,* He thought. *I will give each new soul the ability to choose either me or Lucifer.* He leaned back in His heavenly chair and looked up into the cosmos, thinking. After several minutes of contemplation, God put His heavenly pencil down and said, "This is good. I will call this choice, 'freewill.' I'll give the people on the planet freewill to prove their faith in me as their Father. Yes! That's the ticket. No contracts, just freewill. Although Lucifer has evil intentions, he will be of benefit to My kingdom. Those who reject Lucifer will reveal themselves to Me as faithful. If they choose to follow Lucifer, I will condemn these people to eternal damnation."

So it was that God created the archangels and the multitudes of angels assigned to Planet Earth. Lucifer and his demonic helpers slinked in the shadows, waiting for God's plan to unfold. The dark angel plotted and schemed, preparing for his assault on the new beings once they were born into the new world. When God rested on the seventh day, Lucifer deliberated. Lucifer waited. After the Lord finally created man and woman, the prince of darkness put his game plan into action. God watched intently from His cosmic office as Lucifer approached Eve and convinced her to eat the apple from the tree of the knowledge of good and evil. Lucifer's plan played right into God's hands. Evil was born. Sin followed. And with sin, freewill became its offspring. Lucifer's evil strategy set the Lord's new creation in motion. It was the way God designed it to be. Now it was up to the humans He created to choose. God sat back to watch His followers and waited for them to make their choices.

This fictional tale provides an imaginary scenario of how angels came into existence. This entertaining exercise was written by a nobody and will no doubt invite differing opinions. However, no one can say with absolute certainty it isn't accurate. God didn't think it necessary that we know the finer points of His creation, or it would have been mentioned in the Bible. As Christians, we accept the interpretation of what's available in scripture added to the experiences we've learned through the episodes in life to teach us wisdom. Our faith fills in the gaps.

Angels Appear

The presumption that angels were around at creation is based on somewhat hazy scriptural references, but some theologians agree with this premise. Regardless of their origin, we know from reading God's handbook that angels were prominent characters throughout the Old

Testament. The word "angel" is used 273 times in the Bible, indicating these spiritual beings were like honeybees, flitting about the world, delivering God's messages. One of the first encounters with angels is found in the days of Abraham, written in the book of Genesis. Sarah's maidservant Hagar was offered up to Abraham as a way to conceive an heir. As mentioned in chapter 4, Abraham and Sarah lost patience waiting for a child. When Hagar became pregnant, she despised Sarah. Because of Hagar's feelings, Sarah began mistreating her, and Hagar was finally asked to leave. After departing, an angel came to Hagar in the desert and told her to return and submit herself to Sarah. She was assured that God would increase her descendants too numerous to count. So Hagar returned to Sarah. Years after her return, she and her son Ishmael were cast out again because of the threat of sharing Abraham's inheritance. Mother and son were visited a second time by an angel of God, who helped the two find water and survive in the wilderness.

Abraham was visited by three angels announcing Sarah would become pregnant, and they would have a son. Not long after, Abraham's nephew Lot was rescued by angels from Sodom just before its destruction. Lot followed the angels' guidance and survived, but his wife did not. Abraham's grandson Jacob was no stranger to angels. Angels came to him in his dreams, they met him while he was traveling, and again on his deathbed.

An important event in Jewish history occurred on the night of Passover. The Passover angel brought death to every firstborn of Egyptian families who didn't have blood painted on their doors. This horrible plague was employed by God to convince Pharaoh to let the Israelites leave Egypt. Angels were also present on Mt. Sinai, when God gave Moses the holy tablets. The prophet Balaam was visited by angels of the Lord to warn him he was being disobedient. An angel approached the village of Bochim, not far from the Jordan River, and rebuked the Israelites for making false idols.

God sent an angel to destroy Jerusalem for the Israelites' rampant sinning. Poised to complete the destruction of the city, God stopped the angel from proceeding. Prior to the impending destruction, David saw the angel and spoke to him. Elijah was strengthened by an angel who brought him food and drink. An angel of the Lord killed 185,000 Assyrians after Isaiah predicted to Hezekiah that the Assyrian king, Sennacherib, would be defeated. One of the most vivid accounts of an angel was when Daniel's friends were saved from being burned in a furnace of fire, and later when an angel saved Daniel in the lion's den.

In the New Testament an angel named Gabriel was sent by God to Saint Mary to announce she would have a son. Angels came to the shepherds in their dreams, informing them of the birth of Jesus Christ. Mary Magdalene and Mother Mary were visited by an angel at the open tomb where Jesus was buried, informing the two that Jesus had risen. In Revelation, the apostle John saw an angel who showed him the river of life, and he fell at the feet of the Lord's messenger in reverence.

Angels could be the forerunners of safety and protection, or they could be destroyers bringing doom to the wicked. They served as God's message carriers, His liberators, His executioners, and defenders of His subjects. These heavenly creatures were forerunners of God and always seemed to be at the right place at the right time. Initially angels began appearing in dreams, speaking God's Word. They had the ability to emerge from nowhere, appearing humanlike in form. God occasionally spoke from an angel's body to converse directly with His human subjects.

Types of Angels

According to the Mishneh Torah, angels were ranked from one to ten in importance.[77] Two familiar names within these ranks are seraphims (aka seraphs) and cherubim (aka cherubs). According to a few sources, these angels were higher ranking than the soldier angels.

Because these beings are supernatural, they have an otherworldly presence. All mention of angels lead us to believe they are male creatures, and some are known to have halos. In biblical passages, these angelic souls are described as striking, resembling gems, fine gold, or bronze, or having a face like lightning adorning their image. They are so striking in appearance that for some in the Bible, it was a horrifying experience that struck fear before it was learned they were messengers of God. By some accounts, angels were said to have wings. Whether they had wings or not is debated and could be something Christians have conjured up in our attempts to overdramatize the metaphysical features of God's messengers.

Suffice it to say angels play a pivotal role in God's relationship with His people on earth. We may have heard angels in our dreams orchestrated by the Holy Spirit. They watch over us, like in cases where we avoid certain death and are miraculously saved. Angels may nudge us to do the right thing and tap our shoulders when we're veering off course. Angels can be all around but may not be seen. Each angel serves as the Holy Spirit's emissary and dispatcher. As Christians, we should be aware of these supernatural agents of God and appreciate their roles in our Christian lives.

> Angels shine light into all areas of life ... Helping you to see the light within all! (Melanie Beckler, Christian author[78])

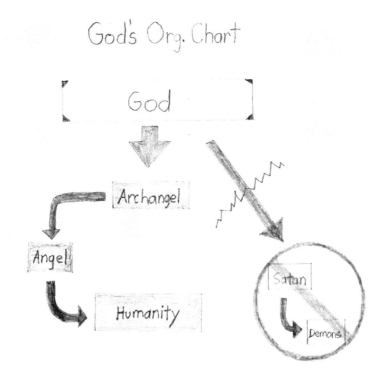

Dear heavenly Father, thank You for sending angels to assist us while on earth. Help us recognize their presence by increasing our awareness and to understand their purpose. Amen.

CHAPTER 19
Devil's in the Details

GOD'S FALLEN ANGEL has lots of names. With a reputation like his, we can imagine all the descriptive appellations concocted over the years. Here's hoping the disrespectful angel who unceremoniously left the kingdom of heaven won't spark revenge on yours truly for writing this chapter. If so, I'll brandish the sword of the Almighty to beat him back into the dark recesses. Some of his aliases are: the Antichrist, Lucifer, Leviathan, the Lawless One, Liar, Ruler of Darkness, Beelzebub, Devil, Belial, Satan, Tempter, Serpent of Old, and the Father of Lies. After departing the Lord's presence, Satan was cursed by God and subjected to dwell in the underworld of hell forever.

A conflict has been underway since God created the angels. Satan has wreaked havoc from the beginning, when Adam and Eve hit the ground in the garden of Eden. From that point forward, Satan became God's antithesis and ran amuck, causing damage, heartache, and mischief. He is the ultimate tempter and seducer. He's cagey, sly, and unpredictable. Lucifer is humanity's plague and has continued to torment God's creatures on earth for centuries. This devilish scourge goes about his dark occupation, spreading evil to all humankind. God continually monitors Satan's activities, and he remains inferior to his Creator. It's thought that God allows Satan to exist primarily to offer His children choices between good and evil. Not surprising, even the letters in the word devil include evil.

Strategy against Satan

When facing an adversary, it's essential to understand their strengths and weaknesses. An understanding of what makes them tick makes the battle less arduous and allows one to develop a strategy. In order for us to circumvent Satan's chicanery, we'll pull back the curtain and dissect his MO.

It's thought that Satan was one of the closest angels to God as described in Ezekiel, where he was anointed as a guardian cherub and ordained by the Lord. He was purported to be one of the most beautiful of all the angels. This led to his pride going unchecked, subsequently corrupting his wisdom (Ezekiel 28:17). When God banished Satan from the heavens, the dark prince led a revolution and added angels to his band of demonic dissenters.

It's important to grasp the idea that Satan is not a fictitious character. He and his forces are *real and powerful*. They must be dealt with seriously and never underestimated. However, the tempter is a defeated angel, and at the end of time, God will pronounce judgment on Satan.

Some critics suggest that Satan doesn't reside in hell but rather lives with us on earth, where he can continually manipulate God's children. Kelly Balarie speaks about Satan's strategies and what he doesn't want us to know. On her blog published on *Crosswalk.com*, Ms. Balarie reveals Satan's propaganda and strategy when attempting to influence our actions.[79]

1. You must fight to win this thing called life.
2. You have no identity.
3. You are not forgiven.
4. God doesn't guide people like you.
5. It's fine if you know God's Word, but you can't know God's love.
6. It's all about your needs.
7. Walk by feelings, not by faith.
8. Live in the past.
9. Fear everything.
10. God can save you for eternity, but He doesn't save you on earth.

Satan's Mission Objectives

What becomes obvious and exposes Satan's scheme is to understand his ability to confuse and distort. He's very adept at baiting us with false teachings and luring us into sin. He wants us to turn against each other, thus divide and conquer. When he's successful at leading us astray, it keeps us from glorifying God. Satan wants our light extinguished, so we won't be able to throw light on his darkness. As seen in numbers 6 and 7 above, Lucifer wants us to become self-reliant, so there's no need for the Lord. By influencing a me-first attitude, we lose our allegiance to God and don't seek His guidance.

To battle the demon of darkness, we can't sit back and be passive when confronted with his designs. We must be aggressive and intentional, taking the fight to Satan, and radiating light into his shadows. A way to disrupt his army of nonbelievers is to evangelize our fellow humankind and bring them out of the cave of despair into God's heavenly domain. Prayer is our best means of defeating the enemy and should be exercised whenever we feel threatened. Satan's goal is to keep us from proclaiming the Word and, therefore, accomplishing how God wants us to live. The ongoing battle we wage has often been termed "spiritual warfare," a most appropriate description of this clash.

THE SCREWTAPE LETTERS

Many think that unfavorable things happen because of bad luck, human nature, or some cosmic force blowing in the wind. This is Satan's cloak of confusion. As seen in his book *The Screwtape Letters,* author C. S. Lewis presents a unique perspective on Satan's approach to manipulation. Lewis does this in a unique, satirical approach by composing a story about the main character, Screwtape. The demon Screwtape is a senior officer in the hierarchy of Lucifer's army and is tasked to train his understudy, a novice by the name of Wormwood. The book shares dialogue between the two as Screwtape gives advice and strategy to Wormwood in hopes of inducing the damnation of a young man, their target. The author gives us unique insight as to the demon's techniques and methods to accomplish their goals. In his "Epigraph," Lewis uses a quote from Martin Luther: "The best way to drive out the devil, if he will not yield to texts of Scripture, is to jeer and flout him, for he cannot bear scorn."[80]

Here's some excerpts from his manuscript revealing Screwtape's methodology as he writes letters counseling his junior demon, Wormwood.

> [O]ur best work is done by keeping things out.
>
> All extremes, except extreme devotion to the Enemy [God], are to be encouraged.

> He [God] cannot "tempt" to virtue as we do to vice.
>
> An ever increasing craving for an ever diminishing pleasure is the formula.
>
> Keep his mind off the plain antithesis between True and False. Nice shadowy expressions.[81]

With his brilliant portrayal of the two characters, Lewis raises our level of consciousness to Satan's approach with the deceit and treachery he inflicts on God's subjects.

In the book, Satan says it's okay for God's subjects to have moderate religion, it's as good as no religion at all. One passage, strangely eerie, clarifies the misconception that people think Satan puts things in their mind, but in reality, Satan does his best work by keeping things out.

As if We Don't Have Enough Problems

Unfortunately we're locked in an ongoing skirmish with the great deceiver. He continually tries to mislead us into thinking we should survive on our own. Chuck Lawless is professor and senior associate dean of the Billy Graham School of Missions, Evangelism, and Church Growth at The Southern Baptist Theological Seminary. He has some valuable insight. Lawless says Satan is not our only problem. The world and its destructive nature, along with the weakness of our flesh, enables Satan to seduce people away from God.[82] The world already has enough problems of its own, so the last thing we need is Satan's intervention. He craftily goes about his pursuits, using the strife around us to further his agenda. With the destructive forces surrounding us, we need to develop defenses against his attacks. We need to reinforce our battlements. We can find instruction on how to do this from Ephesians 6:10–17:

Finally, be strong in the Lord and in his mighty power. Put on the full armor of God so that you can take your stand against Lucifer's schemes. For our struggle is not against flesh and blood, but against the rulers, against the authorities, against the powers of this dark world and against the spiritual forces of evil in the heavenly realms. Therefore put on the full armor of God, so that when the day of evil comes, you may be able to stand your ground, and after you have done everything, to stand. Stand firm then, with the belt of truth buckled around your waist, with the breastplate of righteousness in place, and with your feet fitted with the readiness that comes from the gospel of peace. In addition to all this, take up the shield of faith, with which you can extinguish all the flaming arrows of the evil one. Take the helmet of salvation and the sword of the Spirit, which is the word of God.

How do we know when we're under spiritual attack? Here's some indications:

- Increased temptation and being lured toward something sinful
- Feelings of fear, darkness, or despair
- Confusion, guilt, or loss of focus on God
- Suddenly being confronted with losses, troubles, or suffering
- Physical danger, illness, or attacks

As Christians we should protect ourselves from Satan's infiltration and not allow ourselves to be deceived by his sleuth. We're challenged to rise above his immoral temptations and be cognizant of when we're being manipulated. At the point we realize we're under attack, we should take exception to his chicanery, and react quickly. This is when we fight back with righteousness and focus a light into the depths of his darkness. Once exposed he'll depart and try to find a weaker subject to influence. Let's put on the armor, gird for battle, and don't give in to the villainous evil of Satan.

Protection Strategies to Defeat Satan

- ✓ Receive Christ into our heart.
- ✓ Defend ourselves mentally from being duped by Satan.
- ✓ Read scripture and apply its teachings.
- ✓ Pray earnestly to God.
- ✓ Recognize when we're being attacked by Satan; don't allow him to sneak into our lives.
- ✓ Put on the armor of God; bathe in His righteousness.
- ✓ Preach and teach the gospel to others.

- ✓ Remember our salvation in Jesus Christ.
- ✓ Renounce the wicked one.
- ✓ Abstain from occult practices such as astrology, horoscope, ouija, and Spiritism.

The next time Satan reminds you of your past, remind him of his future. (Matthew Henry[83])

Dear Lord, give us strength to battle the evil forces of Satan. Provide us with the confidence found in Your Word that will illuminate his undertakings and drive out his presence. Amen.

CHAPTER 20
Sin City

ALEXANDR SOLZHENITZYN, A writer, philosopher, and political prisoner, said this about sin: "If only there were evil people somewhere insidiously committing evil deeds, and it were necessary only to separate them from the rest of us and destroy them. But the line dividing good and evil cuts through the heart of every human being."[84]

The Epitome of Sin

Sin, in its most fundamental sense, is not obeying God. However, it can be much more complex. We turn to the origin of the word "sin," which is Greek meaning to miss the mark. It's thought that the concept of missing the mark originated in the Hebrew world, whose archers developed the phrase, *hata sin*, which literally means to miss the center of the target. It's evident how this term came to be applied to faith, for when we sin, we miss the mark. This poor aim can best be seen when our arrows fall short of God's target, the Ten Commandments. It doesn't stop there. We can be compliant and obey all God's commandments, but there's a multitude of sins that may not rise to the level of a commandment yet remain a transgression. These acts expose our weaknesses and lack of morality. If we're immoral individuals, we break God's law instructing us to love our fellow human beings. It's not only major offenses, like 'Thou Shalt Not Kill', that brings about God's judgment. Most biblical critics agree that all sins are the same in the Lord's eyes. An example would be when we purposely cut someone off in traffic. There's certainly no law or commandment against it, but it's not the Christian thing to do. Measuring the severity of an offense isn't at issue. A sin is a sin.

Earthly sin can be traced back to our favorite couple, Adam and Eve. Once Satan convinced Eve to bite the apple, she entered into the shadowy gloom of sin. Then Adam followed her lead. Their transgressions against God set the sin-wheel in motion. This event conceived "original sin." Adam and Eve's sin that day was indulgence and being disobedient to God.

There are several types of sin that can be differentiated by the type and circumstance of the insubordination. Here's a look at the various classifications of sins:

> *Original Sin:* The sinful nature of humankind caused by Adam and Eve.

> *Imputed Sin:* After Adam ate the forbidden fruit, his sin led to an inherent sinful nature in all of humanity. It was handed down to all who followed and is inherent to humankind.

Cardinal Sin: The foundation of all sin and gives birth to every other sin. Heard of the seven deadly sins? Each one represents a cardinal sin. They are:

The Seven Deadly Sins

➔ Gluttony
　➔ Lust
　　➔ Greed
　　　➔ Pride
　　　　➔ Anger/Wrath
　　　　　➔ Envy
　　　　　　➔ Sloth (unwilling to do God's work, indifference)

Most of the seven are self-explanatory and where most other sins originate.

Other types of sin include:

Mortal Sin: The spiritual death of the soul. A mortal sin constitutes a serious offense. The sin is committed with full realization and is deliberate.

Deadly Sin: As we might expect, this is a sin that causes or incurs death.

Venial Sin: A minor infraction, slight in nature but still a sin.

Capital Sin: Personal sins that cause other people to sin.

Social Sin: Committing an act that infringes on others' rights and freedoms.

Commission/Omission

There are two categories of sin. The first is a sin of *commission*. This occurs when our actions in words, thoughts, or deeds commit a sin. An example is stealing a candy bar from the store. This is actively undertaking to commit a sin, thereby constituting a sin of commission.

The other form is a sin of *omission*. This is knowing when we should do something good but refuse to act. An example of a sin of omission would be if we were hiking up a mountain and purposely failed to disclose a dangerous stretch to other hikers. This failure to disclose critical safety information is a blatant sin of omission.

A unique thing about sin is that it can compound, creating a proclivity to sin again. Repetition of sin soon turns into a vice and then morphs into something much more perverse. Sin clouds our judgment and corrupts our discernment between good and evil. Sin is a disease. As it reproduces, it causes greater and greater pain.

The Character of a Sinner

Let's adjust the focus and look a little closer. This is a glimpse of how scripture describes a sinner's character. These traits are found in Proverbs 6:16–19.

- Haughty eyes
- A lying tongue
- Hands that shed innocent blood
- A heart that devises wicked schemes
- Feet that are quick to rush into evil
- A false witness who pours out lies
- A man who stirs up dissension among brothers

Types Of Sin

7 Deadly Sins	Types Of Sin		Traits
Gluttony	Mortal	C O M M I S S I O N ∧ ∨ O M I S S I O N	Haughty Eyes
Lust			Shed Blood
Greed	Capital		Wicked Schemes
Pride			False Witness
Anger	Venial		Lying Tongue
Envy	Deadly		Rush To Evil
Sloth			
	Social		Dissension

From the lineup, notice that only two of the sins above *might* break a commandment, that of shedding innocent blood and being a false witness. Unless the shedding causes death, it too would be absent from the sins listed by the Ten Commandments. No matter how we measure the severity of the sin, God sees each with equal weight. This is cause for concern since we've all been guilty of sinning sometime in the course of our lives. Thankfully we have the opportunity to wipe the slate clean. God knew in His ultimate wisdom that we, as His creations with broken souls, would have trouble living up to both His commandments and subordinate sins. As humans, we were hardwired to sin from the moment the skin of the apple was pierced by Adam and Eve in the garden of Eden.

THE UNFORGIVABLE SIN

Jesus says that most sins are forgivable save one: sins against the Holy Spirit. Examples of this would be blasphemous teachings and influencing others to ignore God. An outspoken atheist would be a good representation.

> And so I tell you, every sin and blasphemy will be forgiven men, but the blasphemy against the Spirit will not be forgiven. Anyone who speaks a word against the Son of Man will be forgiven, but anyone who speaks against the Holy Spirit will not be forgiven … (Matthew 12:31–32)

In this passage, Jesus is quite clear about disrespecting God and warns those who practice this kind of behavior, will receive no forgiveness. Again, it begs the question why anyone would risk his or her eternal existence to speak derogatorily toward God and the Holy Spirit. Could it be because the person feels insecure about their self-worth and becomes prideful? These individuals go out of their way to have others validate their beliefs, so they'll somehow be comforted they're not alone. Misery does love company.

Jesus's Mission on Earth

God sent Jesus on an assignment. The mission was to seek and save the lost. He sought to locate the stray sheep who were unable to help themselves and give them guidance to everlasting life. Believing in Jesus is like standing in a shower with Him spraying down on us, washing the sins away. To do so, we first have to turn on the water, and that's bringing Jesus into our life.

When nailed to the cross, Jesus accepted the punishment *we* deserved. His blood was shed in order that we might find righteousness. In essence, an exchange was proposed. We exchange our sinfulness and eternal demise for spiritual, eternal life. We should take Him up on the offer, now.

The apostle Paul proclaims in Romans 3:22–23, "There is no difference, for all have sinned and fall short of the glory of God," and in Romans 6:23, "For the wages of sin is death, but the gift of God is eternal life in Jesus Christ our Lord."

> Tis no sin to cheat the devil. (Daniel Defoe[5])

> The Bible will keep you from sin, or sin will keep you from the Bible. (Dwight L. Moody[86])

Dear heavenly Father, teach us to be aware of the types of sin and how to steer clear of these troubles. Let us lean on Jesus whenever we falter, so we can be forgiven for our shortcomings. Amen.

CHAPTER 21

Miracles Falling from Above

ARE MIRACLES REAL? What constitutes a miracle? How do we know when a miracle occurs? Is it possible miracles go unnoticed when they happen around us? There are so many unanswered questions about this phenomenon, but somehow we sense when a miracle happens. This is especially true when we're involved or impacted by a miracle. Trying to gain a grasp on the concept requires analysis of its meaning. A miracle is a surprising and welcome event that violates the laws of science or nature. When this occurrence takes place, the explanation generally points to a higher power who caused the phenomenon. As Christians, we believe this is God's work.

Pastor John Hamel makes a presentation on miracles in which he describes four types.[87] I've taken the liberty of paraphrasing his thoughts.

Miracles over Nature

Let's start with some examples that can be found in the various verses within the Bible. There are too many to count, but here's some that stand out:

- Jesus turning water into wine
- Jesus walking on water
- Jesus turning a few fish and loaves of bread into enough to feed thousands
- Daniel saved in the lion's den
- Parting of the Red Sea
- Turning manna to food
- Mary's virgin birth
- The burning bush

God has performed countless miracles over nature, and Jesus learned from His Father.

Miracles over Supply

Pastor Hamel explains this type of miracle is related to provision. Whenever we fall short of resources, food, or daily needs, a miracle happens, and we're given what we need to get by. A good example of this is the ministry my wife oversees. Through the years, we've been supporting teenage boys in Costa Rica with their school expenses, allowing them to receive a better education. There have been times when we didn't have sufficient funding for the coming month's expenses, and miraculously, someone stepped up and made a contribution. This happened time and time again. This is a miracle over supply.

Miracles over Healing

These miracles require little explanation. We've all experienced some miracle of healing. Whether it's a friend or relative who was miraculously healed from an inoperable disease, or someone who sustains a life-threatening injury and somehow recovers. Whenever the opportunity arises, ask a doctor if he or she has ever seen or experienced a miracle. Most will say they have, and there's no scientific explanation. Medical professionals are trained in science and rely on physiological predeterminants that dictate how a human body should react to procedures and medicines. When a patient's body does things that can't be explained, it's a sign God is working behind the scenes. Medical professionals are excellent witnesses to God's handiwork.

My mom was celebrating her thirty-fifth birthday with friends at our house, so several of my buddies and I left and went to the park. We found a creek that wound through a recreational area. I jumped onto a swing made of cable, hanging from a tree that dangled high above a ravine. I fell fifteen feet to the dry creek bed below, and hit my head on a rock. My skull was fractured front to back. I was transported to the hospital and remained in a coma for over a week, struggling for my life. After a few weeks, I began to heal. The doctor told Mom and Dad my recovery was a miracle. The fact that I'm able to write these words now is a living example of God's miracle of healing.

Miracles over Demons

Jesus performed several miracles over demons. Some examples seen in the Bible are when He wouldn't allow Satan to speak. He also cast out demons from those possessed including pigs sent over a steep bank, falling to their death. In scripture the evil one continually tried to usurp and discredit Jesus and His authority, but he always fell short. Satan couldn't hold a candle to His majestic strength.

INSTANTANEOUS VS. LONG TERM

There's little doubt that miracles are real. My experience tells me this firsthand. We've all probably encountered some form of miracle. The proof is found in unexplainable events that defy nature, science, logic, time, or rationale. When evaluating these wonders, we can classify miracles into instantaneous or long term-unfolding over time. Some of the miracles performed by Jesus were instantaneous. There's others that took years and sometimes centuries to blossom into fruition. Consider the martyrdom and deaths of the disciples who taught the Word of Jesus over the years following Jesus's death and resurrection. It's amazing how the efforts of these few dozen individuals two thousand years ago were responsible for what we know today as Christianity. Jesus's miraculous conception, his life, death, and resurrection happened over time. He was a miracle in His own existence. Noah and his family's survival and then repopulating the world and replenishing wildlife on earth were miracles that happened over time. Even the miracle of earth's creation happened over the period of a heavenly week.

A more recent example is our space travel to the moon. *Apollo 11* faced all kinds of problems before successfully landing on the lunar surface. They continually monitored error codes on the console and couldn't get clarification on the problems from ground control. Communication was spotty with Houston, which further confused the situation. The astronauts weren't in the location they were supposed to be for the landing approach. The spacecraft was extremely low on fuel, and the ship developed pressure problems in the engine fuel line. Yet somehow they landed safely, narrowly averting disaster.[88] The US space program took decades to finally land on the moon. This miracle unfolded over time and brought the entire world together in the process. Simultaneous to the long-term miracle that was revealed, the instant miracle occurred when *Apollo* 11's improbable landing became reality.

GOD'S PLAN FOR MIRACLES

Why are there miracles? A few reasons come to mind. First and foremost, miracles are used to glorify God and make us aware of His power in our lives. We should be grateful for His interventions in our world, including those around us who are involved in these supernatural events. Miracles also confirm God's message of the truths He proclaims. Additionally, the Lord intercedes on our behalf to better our circumstances or help us with problems. Miracles are a way for God to lead humankind to trust in His existence. The act of miracles is God's ammunition, deployed to bring endurance to His Word and bring faith to believers and those who are yet to find true meaning in the Lord.

IT'S A GOD THING

We've probably heard this saying many times. The shorthand for this term is a miracle. Whenever this phrase is spoken, we might discount whatever happened as just a really cool thing or a coincidence. However, as these events do take place, we should stop and appreciate what occurred. We might gloss right over it and give it a smile. But these are the times we need to stop and thank God earnestly for what He's done. Some common occurrences we see often, are random people brought together miraculously to accomplish a common goal, or when things suddenly fall into place out of disarray. Being at "the right place at the right time"; ever hear that one? Or how about, "I don't know why they chose me," or, "Wow, that was really a close call"? Let's not take these episodes lightly. Give thanks, and praise God for revealing Himself to us through miracles.

> A miracle is an event which creates faith. That is the purpose and nature of miracles. Frauds deceive. An event which creates faith does not deceive: therefore it is not a fraud, but a miracle. (George Bernard Shaw[89])

Lord, we see miracles all around us. Help us appreciate the small miracles and to be grateful when You show Yourself through these inexplicable actions. Let us use miracles to glorify You and Your Son, Jesus Christ. Amen.

CHAPTER 22
Who's Foolin' Whom?

WHEN I WAS a kid, my older sister warned me never to call someone a fool. If I did, she said, "You'll go to hell." The point was made, and I avoided using this term for fear of wallowing in the abyss of torment for the rest of my life. This mysterious term "fool" played havoc in my head for many years thereafter. What constitutes a fool? A person who is unwise; yes, that makes sense. Someone who is silly or imprudent; jot those down too. We have many terms for a fool—blockhead, dunce, dolt, ignoramus, imbecile, cretin, dullard, simpleton, moron, clod, nitwit, halfwit, dope, ninny, nincompoop, chump, dimwit, dingbat, dipstick, goober, coot, goon, dumbo, dummy, ditz, dumdum, fathead, butthead, numbskull, knucklehead, dunderhead, thickhead, airhead, flake, lamebrain, mouth-breather, zombie, nerd, peabrain, birdbrain, scissorbill, jughead, jerk, donkey, twit, goat, dork, twerp, lamer, schmuck, bozo, boob, turkey, schlep, chowderhead, dumbhead, goofball, goof, goofus, doofus, hoser, galoot, lummox, knuckle-dragger, klutz, putz, sap, meatball, dumb cluck, or mook. I'm sure there are others.

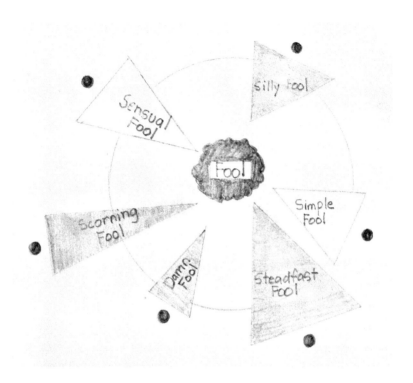

FOOL VS. FOOLISHNESS

The Bible has something to say about fools. It uses the term over a hundred times, so there must be a reason. Fool is used in contrast to a person who shows wisdom. God loves wisdom. Foolishness not so much. The biblical version of fool isn't defined as we would today in our vocabulary. The scriptural term for fool has nothing to do with a person's intelligence quotient. Rather, it's a state of mind and describes a person's character. If we extrapolate meaning from that perspective, it's someone who lacks biblical wisdom or respect for God and His righteousness. When mentioned in the Old and New Testaments, a fool is therefore translated as someone who lacks respect for God.

> As a dog returns to vomit, so a fool repeats his folly.
> (Proverbs 26:11)

Description of a Fool

We can understand the preceding verse to mean that fools do not learn from their mistakes. They continue doing the same foolish things over and over again, moving closer to their downfalls. Here are some excerpts from the Bible describing a fool.

- Hates knowledge
- Takes no pleasure in understanding
- Enjoys wicked schemes
- Proclaims folly
- Speaks perversely
- Quick-tempered
- Speaks proudly
- Mocks sin
- Is deceitful
- Despises his mother
- Brings grief to his or her parents
- Is sexually immoral
- Tears down his or her own house

The term "fool" that my sister was referring to was when Christ forbade calling someone *raca*. This is yesteryear's version of the word "fool." He insisted that we should never do this since it meant the person was beyond the reach of God and would be condemned forever. This didn't mean we can't call someone foolish. Two different things.

Types of Fools

Here we describe six types of fools, most of which are from a biblical perspective.

Simple Fool: This is someone who lacks discernment and opens their heart and mind to any passing thought or feeling.

Silly Fool: A silly fool is someone who spouts off meaningless thoughts and is a human run-on sentence. This person often ignores instruction, doesn't listen well, and becomes upset when things go wrong.

Sensual Fool: This variety hates authority and doesn't like being managed. He or she seems determined to make all the wrong choices.

Scorning Fool: As the adjective describes, this is someone who can't hide his or her emotions and goes around scowling and giving off negative vibes. To God this shows contempt for Him and others.

Steadfast Fool: This particular version is the most perilous and could even be considered wicked. This person tends to be overconfident and proud. The person tries to drag others down to his or her level. The steadfast fool doesn't sense that he or she needs God and touts his or her own authority.

Damn Fool: Okay, this one I added. Everyone in Texas knows what this means.

When confronted with one of the five S-fools, what do we do? Proverbs 26:4 advises us to keep quiet and not confront a fool, or we risk becoming a fool ourselves. We shouldn't let ourselves be dragged into disagreements that are futile and cause us to alienate one other. Staying silent is sometimes the best reply to someone acting or speaking foolishly. Never enter into a disagreement with a fool when we're angry.

Social Media

There's a lot of foolishness on social media these days, especially around the time of the election in 2020. I've never seen such childish behavior and resultant division in our country. We're encouraged to speak our minds on these sites, and those who did were generally acting as mouthpieces for whatever news service they watched. This happened on both sides, Democrat and Republican. It seems most news services are loaded with editorial comments, innuendos, and what I call falsetto news. Falsetto news is part fact, part editorial, and part sensationalism. We should never base our thoughts and ideas on what's heard from some of these sources. In many cases, they're irresponsible at best.

At times we're lured into disagreements on social media. When someone makes an outlandish comment, we feel it necessary to respond to defend our perspective, or perhaps the perspective we've been brainwashed into believing. What follows is a sudden escalation, and hatred boils over onto the combatants as malicious messages go back and forth. God does not like what's appearing on these sites.

> A fool finds no pleasure in understanding but delights in airing his own opinions. (Proverbs 18:2)

> He who answers before listening—that is his folly and his shame. (Proverbs 18:13)

It's not a Christian response to quarrel and argue. Having a difference of opinion is one thing. Making personal attacks is not okay. We can exacerbate the situation using the internet to embolden our positions because we aren't in the same room or face-to-face with the other person. Suffice it to say that even though there's some good on these sites, the trend is turning us into isolationists, separatists, antagonists, and pugilists. We seem to be moving further and further away from God's calling.

Email

Emailing can also lead to misunderstandings. Many thoughts and expressions written foolishly can be misconstrued when deciphering an email. This type of communication sometimes lacks authentic dialogue and understanding. A message that seems curt to the recipient may not have been intended that way, but it registered with them as being impolite. As Christians, there's a lot expected of us. If there's a communication impasse, we need to pick up the phone. Don't be a fool and continue frivolous dialogue that leads to hard feelings. To combat this phenomenon, successful businesses suggest that whenever there's an important email with no rush to send it, let it sit overnight. That way our feelings when writing are set aside. When returning to it the next day, we may see things in a different light. Sending an edgy email late at night lacks wisdom. Attacking someone or trying to put someone in their place is irresponsible. This holds true for texts as well, if not more so. Messaging can be truncated and abbreviated, which can lead to confusion and misunderstanding. These services are great, and I'd find it hard to live without them. But Christian decorum should be the order of the day. We need to use these means of communication with wisdom, not foolishness.

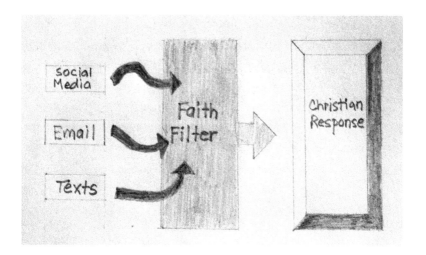

When we're confronted by someone speaking foolishly, what should we do?

Responding to Foolishness

Let's repeat the strategy of silence. Reacting to someone who's said or done something foolish channels us into that person's domain. If we engage in this type of discussion, we're walking into a minefield, right where they want us. We've been successfully seduced into an entanglement in which the other person is probably more adept at this hand-to-hand combat. Some people excel at this game and want nothing more than for us to lower ourselves to their levels so they can legitimize their positions. It's especially important to avoid these situations if it's a casual acquaintance or someone we don't know. Nothing productive will come from these confrontations.

If the relationship with a friend or family member is of value and there's a desire to maintain a civil relationship, there's a right way to go about addressing foolish statements and discussions. We might find it necessary to speak up. This is especially true when the person is entering into territory that's factually incorrect, evil, or lacks civility. The individual needs to hear the truth, and if we're confident of the truth, we should speak up so they won't continue down a path detrimental to their soul. Anger is honey to Satan. Indignant words are useless and should never be an option for rebuttal. My dad always stressed the need to be cool, calm, and collected. There's no better advice to deploy in these situations.

> The tongue has the power of life and death. (Proverbs 18:21)

When we're under control and tranquil, we can think straight and communicate more effectively. This allows us to be more composed and more authentic with what we intend to say. The other person should notice the lack of aggression and sense our compassion and empathy. Rather than alienating the person with our reply, this may open channels to improve the exchange.

One night at college I was asleep in my dorm room when a friend burst through the door, ranting and raving. Apparently someone had wronged him, and he assumed I was the culprit. Guilty of many things in college, that night I was innocent for a change. He was in a rage and wanted to fight. Instinctively, or perhaps because I was half asleep, I slowly propped myself up on my elbows. Looking him in the eye, I elicited Dad's calm, cool, and collected advice and peacefully explained I didn't know what he was talking about. The anger escaped his body, and I could hear him exhale a sigh of remorse for making the accusation. My friend sat on the bed, put his hands on his face, and began weeping. He was hurting. How different would things have turned out if I hopped out of bed and challenged his accusation? Like an aircraft, we must always have our navigation under control.

> [A]nd we take captive every thought to make it obedient to Christ. (2 Corinthians 10:5)

When disagreement looms, decide whether the undertaking is worthwhile. If the subject is important to one's faith or safety, it may be time to challenge the other person's position. From time to time the disciples rebuked each other when a brother needed guidance, and they weren't afraid to correct each other. Stated with kindness and sincerity, the rebuke will be more effective. Before crafting our response, we need to be certain of our motives. Best idea is to run them through our compassion filter, check our hearts, and then open our mouths to speak.

Foolishness is contagious. Don't self-inflict the infection by encouraging this type of behavior. Impart wisdom and be cool, calm, and collected. How we handle ourselves in these situations will define our identities.

> It's better to keep your mouth closed and let people think you are a fool than to open it and remove all doubt. (Mark Twain[90])

Dear Lord, guide us when confronted by foolishness. We need Your peace and wisdom to avoid disagreements. Stop us when we approach the threshold of foolish behavior. Give us compassion and discernment. Amen.

CHAPTER 23
Food for Thought

FOOD SERVED AT meals provides sustenance for us as human beings. Without eating we would soon perish. God's physical design of our bodies makes ingesting food the single most important function we carry out in maintaining our existence. Over the millennia, the ceremonial tradition of meals was conceived to represent significant milestones with our families, associates and friends.

The essential process of eating with others continues to show more benefits than any other assembly we conduct in our daily lives. First, let's look at families who take meals together. See what researchers have substantiated about families who regularly share meals and have opportunities to come together:

→ Strengthens the family unit
→ Builds on household relationships

- → Develops a sense of belonging (which leads to greater self-esteem)
- → Offers parents an opportunity to be role models (can set examples for good table manners and healthy eating)[91]

In research studies, it was found that a family meal:

- → Is generally more nutritious and well rounded
- → Has a greater variety of foods and tends to lead those around the table to be less picky
- → Helps prevent obesity; the family setting encourages slower eating and more talking
- → Discourages high-risk behaviors such as substance abuse and violence
- → Lowers the chances of developing psychological problems[92]

Family meals bring together distant relatives, help reconnect estranged family members, and strengthens relationships within the clan. It gives those around the table a chance to hear each other's concerns and celebrate their joys. It's a time for commemorating birthdays, graduations, weddings, and other special occasions. These gatherings bring families closer, and we get to share life's memories together. Fond recollections punctuate the special times we celebrate our family meals during Easter, Thanksgiving, Fourth of July, and Christmas, which are some of the most memorable.

Beyond time with family, meals and sharing the table has consistently brought people together with, more often than not, good results. There's something about the time together that creates an intrinsic bond with the person across the table. The guests embark on a new union and association. It gives each party a chance to unwind and discuss personal feelings, beliefs, interests, and initiatives. Satisfying the primal need of hunger over a meal allows each person to enter the other individual's window of existence. That's why business lunches are so valuable to a successful sales call or a company venture. A corporate meal can develop strategy, build morale, increase productivity, and encourage teamwork and unity. There are countless situations that create goodwill when breaking bread together. Whether it's dinner on a first date, a youth sports team celebration, a pizza party with neighbors, or a barbecue with workmates, each serves as a communal fusion vital to our existences.

It's no wonder God and the authors of the books of the Bible place so much importance on the act of dining. There are hundreds of references within the scriptures that talk about food, meals, and eating. The Bible barely begins when, in Genesis 3:6–7, we find the first mention of eating, with Adam and Eve consuming the forbidden fruit. This sequence sets the table, so to speak, for circumstances that occur around meals where sustenance is taken. Some other iconic examples familiar to most Christians are noted to underscore the importance:

- The tax collector named Levi who met Jesus, was asked to follow him. This resulted in Levi holding a great banquet for Jesus at his house (Luke 5:27–29).
- A Pharisee invited Jesus to his home for a dinner. While there, a sinful woman appeared and anointed Jesus with perfume (Luke 7:36–39).
- Jacob negotiated with Esau over a bowl of stew to gain his older brother's birthright (Genesis 25:29–34).
- Jacob fed his father, Isaac, some tasty food on his deathbed masquerading as his brother Esau to gain his sibling's blessing (Genesis 27:1–30).
- God conveys what food is unclean and that which is acceptable. He makes it quite clear the importance of the food one should consume to remain holy. This emphasizes the critical nature

of food as it relates to our spiritual health (Genesis, Leviticus, and Deuteronomy).
- The Passover meal originated to commemorate the mercy of God sparing the Israelites from the plague of death directed at the firstborn sons of Egypt. Jesus celebrated this tradition at possibly the most pivotal meal in history, the Last Supper (Leviticus 23:4–8).
- The seven-day feast commencing Passover alongside the Feast of Unleavened Bread (Leviticus 23:26).
- At Pentecost people were traditionally expected to bring the first harvest of grain to the Lord, including two loaves of unleavened bread (Leviticus 23:16).
- Jesus knew how important it was to feed those who were waiting to hear Him speak, and through miraculous means, He turned a few loaves of bread and a few fish into enough to feed over five thousand (John 6:1–13).
- At the wedding celebration in Cana, Jesus performed His first miracle, turning water into wine (John 2:1–11).
- Lastly, Jesus used a metaphor with Peter, instructing him to teach and lead His followers to faith. He told him to "Feed my sheep" (John 21:17).

When we focus on meals and eating in the Bible, the importance that God places on this ritual is apparent. It's evident Jesus used mealtime for inviting unwanted guests or outcasts, to heal the sick, to feed the hungry, or to dine with His enemies. It was a means to accomplish His purpose on earth. It's no wonder tradition leads us to pray before meals because it's likely the most poignant time to reach out to God prior to addressing our physical nourishment.

To conclude the discussion on meals, we should undoubtedly celebrate the essential act of provision when taking communion at church. It was said, "Take and eat; this is my body," and, "Drink from it, all of you. This is my blood of the covenant which is poured out for many for the forgiveness of sins" (Matthew 26:26–28).

Now that we know the importance that God and His Son place on feeding ourselves as well as others, it becomes apparent why fasting is an integral form of worship.

Fasting

Lent is a period of penance that prepares us for celebrating Easter. It begins on Ash Wednesday, six and a half weeks before the most important Sunday in the year. Lent provides for a forty-day fast that imitates Jesus's fasting in the wilderness before He began His public ministry. Why did Jesus fast? We understand this was His way of preparing Himself to commune with God and to build strength against Satan and his temptations.

So why do we fast? For many of the same reasons. We do this to commune with God, build strength, and to prioritize what is most important to our survival. As Christians, we sacrifice feeding ourselves, which becomes secondary to that of being with the Lord. Fasting is not so much about suffering and giving up something of value. It is more about exchanging food or some other valuable commodity to make more room for God. It has many benefits. Award-winning author Brooke Obie says:

1. A soul cleansing … Fasting is a great time to remember the spiritual connection we have to our physical bodies.
2. A new desire for God. When we acknowledge through fasting that we need God to *live*, and to live more abundantly, we can begin to desire God in a new way.
3. A deeper praise. Because the body does not have to do the work of digestion, it has more energy to focus on other things … we have more energy to devote to God.

4. A sensitivity to God's voice … When we detox the spirit and become consumed with desire and praise for God, we become sensitive to His voice.
5. A new satisfaction. When you finish your fast, renewed, full of energy, detoxed, with a new desire, a new praise and a sensitivity to God's voice, you'll find that the absence of food was small in comparison to what you gained.[93]

> Physical food never fully satisfies; in a few hours you'll need to eat again. But when you are fed from doing the work of the Lord, you will find a new satisfaction like you've never experienced. (Brooke Obie[94])

We fast for a number of the reasons mentioned here, but it boils down to practicing self-control and adhering to a commitment. This takes effort and perseverance. It opens the floodgates, so God can flow into our lives, and we can hear Him clearly and sense His presence. It gives us the opportunity to bare our souls, admit our shortcomings—including our sins and our brokenness. This also indicates our reliance on the Father and helps us to think more clearly without distraction. The brain retains all the blood flow without sacrificing vital energy that would otherwise be directed to the stomach for digesting food. Experts call this "mental acuity."

Fasting was originally designed for abstaining from food in general. In modern-day versions, it may pertain to certain foods or fasts that are of the non-edible variety. We can fast from social media, sugar, drinking alcohol or smoking cigarettes. We can even fast from shopping. There are any number of ways to fast. However, the purpose of a legitimate fast is to withhold use or consumption of something we value and that is vital to our personal desires. This commitment indicates to God where our priorities lie. Personally, I have a predilection for music. So much so that it becomes a focus sometimes rather than a nonessential dimension of my life. Ten years ago, I committed to forgo music on Sundays as my way of fasting and showing reverence to God. The one exception, of course, is listening to worship music at church.

One of the most critical aspects of a fast is how good it feels. We've honored an obligation and arrive at the end of a fast knowing we held up our end of the bargain. We did what we said we would do. God sees this dedication and observes our desire to honor Him in this way. The ultimate banquet is yet to come, when there will be no fasting, and we'll get to enjoy the fruits of our labors in heaven. We can look back with pride knowing that our fasts on earth were but small sacrifices for eternal life.

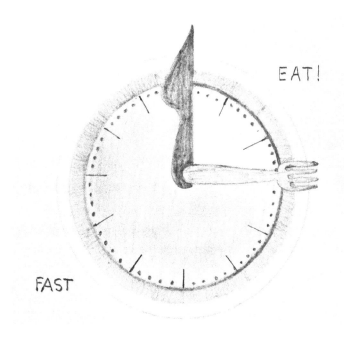

Father God, teach us the benefits of fasting, and give us the devotion to carry through with our commitment to bring us closer to You. Amen.

CHAPTER 24
Idol Time

THIS IS GOING to be painful and difficult to digest. Take a seat, let's put on a crash helmet, and buckle the safety belt. Strap in and brace for impact.

Most of us don't think we have any idols. As we'll find out, there are many; some we may not have considered idols. Eons ago, pagan idols and craven images were worshipped instead of God. These could be the sky, the moon, the sun, precious metals, statues, animals, stones, rain; the list is infinite. There was a random god on every corner. The Greeks worshipped twelve gods and goddesses. Throw in the Olympian gods, and it would take a spreadsheet to understand who to worship and when. These false idols from ancient times are but vintage models of what we worship today. Idols have been around since God created humankind, and although the characteristics have changed, they still have the same implications.

Idolatry Up Close

The essence of idolatry is shifting our focus from God and resting it on something temporal and nonspiritual. Whatever we value more than God and whatever influences our thinking is considered an idol. The need for an alternative to God is usually associated with personal pride. Greed, fame, gluttony, and love for possessions are some examples. These false idols discourage us from concentrating on the Lord, who requires our faithfulness to Him, not objects.

Does God wants us to worship objects or false gods that virtually take the front seat while He rides quietly in the back? Certainly not. The first commandment is, "You shall have no other gods before me" (Exodus 20:3).

If that wasn't clear enough, He wanted to make sure we were listening when the second commandment was written: "You shall not make for yourself an idol in the form of anything in heaven above or on the earth beneath or in the waters below. You shall not bow down to them or worship them; for I the Lord your God, am a jealous God" (Exodus 20:4).

Message heard loud and clear. But how easy it is to wander from our good intentions. We're all flawed. We are human after all, prone to err. Idolizing is one area where we can never be too careful. I'm guilty of disobeying these commandments occasionally without realizing it until later. Other times I blatantly disregard the commandments, thinking it doesn't apply to whatever I'm worshipping on a given day. *Oh, this is really isn't worshipping,* I might think. It seems that we're attracted to the latest, newest, or shiniest object that stimulates our minds' consciousness. The important point here is whatever the interest is, it shouldn't be elevated to a primary level of importance. Never should it be greater than our relationship with God. What it boils down to is the constant battle with the idol of self. This is our old nemesis, pride.

Our society is becoming more and more self-obsessed. We become our own idols. Instinctively we ask ourselves, "How will this affect me?" "What's in it for me?" "What can I gain from this?" "This is my time, and I'll do with it what I want." We're all guilty of this. Most behavior that crosses the line can be traced to some sort of insecurity, whether it be relationships, success, approval, health, food, comfort, or intellect.

Jeremy Edgar, who is better known online as the Canadian Bible Guy, shares some compelling insights about idols. The blogger identifies three major types of idolatry.[95]

Pagan Idolatry

Edgar explains that pagan idolatry is probably the easiest to recognize. It brings to mind rituals or mysterious observances praising some arbitrary deity. Pagan worship is ceremonial, and followers worship some object of spirituality, obviously not God. Although paganism is an antiquated form of worshipping, it still exists in familiar practices. Yoga, in its truest form, is an example. Edgar lists another example like transcendental meditation, associated with Hinduism and Buddhism.

Secular Idolatry

Edgar categorizes secular idolatry as that which doesn't involve God or anything spiritual. This practice usually involves worshipping cultural gods like money, romance, success, food, image, sex, collections, physical appearance, hobbies, relationships, and a plethora of other things. Those cursed with OCD, which includes me as a club member, have to be especially careful since we're driven to practice these secular rituals, repetitively and excessively. A few years ago I bought a few cacti and became obsessed with the how easy they were to grow. Before blinking an eye, I had over three hundred pots of cacti and succulents. I began transplanting, reproducing, and selling them; it got out of hand quickly. Now it's obvious how far off the grid I wandered and how cactus became a secular idol. I was forgoing good judgment to sustain the passion I mistakenly felt was necessary. Excess is an abscess.

Religious Idolatry

I have to admit Edgar threw me a curve on this one. Religious idolatry is not what I expected it to be. He explains that someone can go through the rituals, attend church, make offerings, take communion, and sing the hymns but fail to worship God with the heart. This is committing religious idolatry. The Lord would undoubtedly be frustrated with these individuals who are attending worship, immersed in His presence, but they don't commit themselves fully to Jesus Christ.

Exit Our Idols

God calls each of us to rid ourselves of idols, no matter the type. The first measure in doing so is recognition. We need to admit that we have idols, like when I finally woke up and saw the succulent collection for what it was. Sometimes it takes an awakening to jolt ourselves into awareness. We should closely inspect our lives and daily rituals as someone might from the outside looking in. We should ask ourselves, "Does what I'm doing appear abnormal or excessive? Do I worship this object? Is it an idol?"

Once we identify idols in our lifestyle, we should wean ourselves away. We should change, rearrange, reprioritize, and normalize. A second step is to ask God's forgiveness for failing to heed His commandment. Once forgiven, which is certain to happen we can establish mental borders to stay within. It's time to take authority of our lives and not let material idols consume our world.

> Whatever your heart clings to and confides in, that is really your God, your functional savior. (Martin Luther[95])

> Nothing teaches us about the preciousness of the Creator as much as when we learn the emptiness of everything else. (Charles Spurgeon[97])

Dear God, make us aware of the idols we have in our lives. Give us strength to put them aside and keep You at the center of our thoughts and be our only true God. Amen

CHAPTER 25
In Union We Stand; in Division We Fail

WHY DO WE attend church? Out of obligation? To check a box? To do the right thing? Attending church is so much more. Worshipping God with one another may be one of the most important things we can do as Christians. In the following paragraphs, we explore the benefits of corporate worship, which are numerous and integral to our faith.

REKINDLING THE FLAME

Worshipping together not only lights the fire of faith, it *keeps* the fire burning. As individuals, we thrive in a relational world. Without others we would become depressed, anxious, and isolated. God made us communal; that was His design.

Community Dynamics

When we worship alone, we miss the collective enthusiasm of other Christians. As the masses gather, one gets a feeling of unity. We become part of a brotherhood, not unlike what we would experience at a sporting event. When we're surrounded by fans equally as passionate about our favorite team, there's an unspoken euphoria that pervades the senses through this connection. We're lifted, we're energized, our adrenaline escalates. We get a visceral high that's very hard to explain. The same phenomenon occurs at church. When those around us are pulling for the same team, there's a synergy and a common purpose. From this unity, trust is developed. It's a special feeling when those around us are like-minded. Hope is a product of the common purpose; it buoys our enthusiasm and makes us feel good.

We've all heard the phrase, "strength in numbers." This is unquestionably true in the case of the church body. Let's call this phenomenon "community dynamics." What's meant by dynamics in this context is when people come together, it has a domino effect, spreading far beyond the epicenter. The reaction affects those in attendance as well as others outside the church. These factors provide a multitude of benefits, some of which can't be measured and may not even be consciously realized. Understanding these dynamics is like catching lightning in a bottle. When we attend worship together in a corporate setting, we engage in a shared objective, that of worshiping God through fellowship. Fellowship is made up of a series of elements brought about by the community dynamic.

Fellowship Is Teamwork

It's important to take the time to explore the obvious and subtle components of fellowship. It's been said by biblical scholars that many of God's blessings can only be realized when meeting together. Scripture tells us that the church is Christ's body, so it stands to reason that by attending church, we're inhabiting Christ's metaphorical flesh and bones. Jesus desires for us to take part in worshipping with others. He wants us assembled to glorify His name. We can enjoy three basic benefits from worshipping together. We can hear *His* voice. God can hear *our* voices through prayer and song, and we can belong to *His* body.

As we break down the meaning of a church body, it comes back to fellowship. The term "fellowship" constitutes a wide-ranging collection of actions that produce positive outcomes. In fellowship we find comfort and strength by attending church consistently. We're given the opportunity to share our challenges with others and they with us. This in turn creates relationships based on truth and trust. Hearing opinions and ideas advances our personal growth and broadens our understanding. Our fellow worshippers can offer encouragement and direction by sharing their personal experiences. We learn together as we worship together. This couldn't happen without community.

Worshipping is not limited to attending services each week. It includes fellowshipping through Bible studies, Sunday school, fundraisers, mission projects, and other special events organized by the church. In essence, we become part of a team with like-minded goals and ideas. As these opportunities come about, it's evident more can be accomplished. More people can be strengthened, more individuals can be comforted in times of need, and more people can become accountable to their peers. Encouragement, empathy, comfort, accountability, consolation, knowledge, and relationships are all by-products of worshipping together in fellowship.

It doesn't end there. Togetherness allows us to hear other peoples' testimonies about how they came to Christ. It enlightens us to situations we would never have been exposed to otherwise. We learn ways to live wisely where good examples are made visible for us to follow. As worshippers, we can learn new ways to meditate and pray. We meet new people. We study God's Word and learn biblical truths through the historical accounts written by the prophets, disciples, and apostles. We can lay out our biggest troubles and fears without hesitancy, confident we won't be judged. So much can be achieved from corporate worship, and as our faith grows stronger, it undeniably extends to our families, workplaces, and communities.

> If you're not praying with other believers, then you're not getting the support you need. You're missing out on one of the major benefits of being a Christian. (Rick Warren[98])

> [I]t is impossible, unnecessary, and undesirable to be a Christian all by yourself as it is a newborn baby all by yourself. (Bishop N. T. Wright[99])

When reading about teamwork from a secular perspective, consulting firms describe some of the benefits, including how teamwork builds complementary strengths, teamwork builds trust, teamwork develops conflict-resolution skills, teamwork promotes a wider sense of ownership, and teamwork encourages healthy risk-taking. The same holds true when a church family comes together.

Why Not Worship in Church?

With so much to gain by worshipping in community, why would someone choose not to go to church? Some suggest, "My relationship with God is very personal, and I don't need anyone else but me and the Lord." Some may prefer to worship alone and in solitude. But is this healthy from a Christian perspective? God doesn't think so.

There are many reasons those who consider themselves Christians don't attend worship services. They might not think there's a good reason to go or may be unaware of the many benefits that come from community worship. People at times tend to be unsure and noncommittal. They might think it's a waste of time, whereas they could do more enjoyable things, like prepare for work, cook, play games, enjoy hobbies, be with family, listen to music, relax, or watch TV. Some might say, "I don't have the time," "It's raining," "I don't want to get dressed up," "I don't feel well," "I don't want to shave," "I want to sleep in," "I went last week," "those at church are hypocrites," "it's freezing in the sanctuary," or, "I don't have anything to wear." Or perhaps some may have had bad experiences at church that left a bitter taste, and they've given up the practice altogether. These reasons indicate folks are disillusioned with the purpose of going to church.

ANNUAL REVIEW

Imagine receiving an annual review as we would at work. We sit across from God, who is behind His celestial desk, to go over last year's accomplishments. He looks over our achievements, and there's a glaring issue with church attendance. The Lord asks, "Why didn't you go to church and worship? Don't you know that's one of the most important things I ask?" We hem and haw and then give some of the excuses previously mentioned. God leans over and pulls out the procedure manual from His drawer and reads the guidelines from Hebrews 10:25: "Let us not give up meeting together, as some are in the habit of doing, but let us encourage one another—and all the more as you see the Day approaching."

We leave God's office disappointed. There were satisfactory marks in just about every area of being a good Christian until it came to attending church. God listed this as a weakness and issued a "needs improvement" rating. Because of our questionable judgment, we didn't get a promotion.

Are We Leading or Is God?

Over time, many have evolved into self-seeking individuals. Some have a strong desire to manage their own lives and can't see beyond the penchant to run the show. Some Christians, try to initiate their worship rather than to receive it. They'll decide when to worship, when and how to pray, what verses to read and what songs to sing. This runs smoothly as long as they are in control. According to David Mathis, executive editor of *desiringGod.org*, we should be receptors, not initiators. He says we should position ourselves to receive and thus be *led* in worship. This way is more pleasing to God. Let's take our hands off the wheel, and let God guide our paths.[100]

> [A]t home, in my own house, there is no warmth or vigor in me, but in the church when the multitude is gathered together, a fire is kindled in my heart and it breaks its way through. (Martin Luther[101])

At times we can feel like we're in a spiritual fog and disoriented with our worship experiences. If so, it could be that we're being too legalistic—excessively adhering to the worship tradition—or the other extreme, just going through the motions. It may be time to harness the power of good habits. The United Methodist Church through its founder, John Wesley believes in the Wesleyan Quadrilateral *method*ology. This means developing good habits in worship, wherein the Methodist name is derived. Foundational beliefs of the Methodist faith are scripture, tradition, reason, and the Christian experience. Both tradition and the Christian experience point to our worship rituals.

Our worship services should be productive experiences, where habits are developed, influenced by tradition.

Why Worship at Church, Revisited

Let's pose the question again: Why not attend church? In response, the following list should be enough to convince anyone who doesn't attend regularly how essential it is to worship together. It offers these benefits:

*Scripture interpretation	*Finding comfort	*Accountability
*Finding strength	*Power of collective prayer	*Personal growth
*Team accomplishments	*Build stronger faith	*Enhanced worship
*Consolation when in need	*Receive God's blessings	*Develop relationships
*Share knowledge and insight	*Learn of good acts	*Hear testimonies
*Group mission projects	*Expand godly IQ	*Help others
*Way of salvation	*Set good example for kids	*Sing inspirationally
*Awe accentuated	*Adoration increased	*Find joy
*Hear other opinions	*Souls rescued	

Bottom line: Go to church and worship. Let us be receptive to the Word, and let God's presence flow over us. Be habitual, be consistent, and don't make excuses to stay at home. Be flexible to change, embrace fellowship, and join the community of believers. Then enjoy the fruits.

But as for me, it is good to be near God. (Psalm 73:28)

Dear God, help us to keep the fire burning for worshipping together and to be present when Your Word is spoken. Let us enter into fellowship with our brothers and sisters in Christ. Amen.

CHAPTER 26
What Really Matters

MUCH HAS BEEN made lately about Blue Lives Matter, Black Lives Matter, and White Lives Matter. I contend that *every* life matters. The last few years have proven to be downright shameful in the history of our great country. Not since the sixties has America shown its disgusting and embarrassing identity like it has in recent times. What progress had been made with racial inequities over the last half century seems to have been wiped out in a matter of a few years. We've taken a giant step backwards in our efforts to level the playing field. Our Black brothers and sisters still face ongoing disparagement, bias, prejudice, and bigotry. As a member of the White race, I see a continuation of this behavior, only now it's cleverly disguised and camouflaged.

> **NEW**
> **J's CAFETERIA**
> 350 SEATS - 3 LG. DINING ROOMS
> NEW SPEED LINE SERVICE
> QUALITY FOOD-REASONABLE PRICES
> 5025 LEMMON AVE. NEAR INWOOD
> DALLAS TEXAS
> NOW OPEN 7 DAYS A WEEK

Cafeteria Education

Fortune blessed me to be the son of a cafeteria owner. When old enough to work, I was commissioned to be employed at one of the stores. The surroundings were undoubtedly foreign to me when arriving. At the cafeteria, I was thrust into a different world that was puzzling and a little unnerving. The employees at the cafeteria were all Black. It goes without saying that I didn't fit in. There was a lot of suspicion, distrust, and discomfort on both sides. When I arrived, the workers had to stomach a wet behind the ears, young White man who invaded their presence. Even worse, I was the owner's son, which added a second layer of vexation. The employees treated me cordially, but in no way was I accepted and I certainly wasn't trusted.

I was an observant young student of human nature. The workers' attitudes toward me didn't go unnoticed. After a week or so, there was a need on my part to gain their trust. This wasn't easy. Being the owner's son didn't make me feel comfortable around the employees any more than they were comfortable around me. As time went on, things happened in the kitchen that the owner or managers wouldn't have tolerated. Perhaps they were testing me. Food was eaten from what was prepared, and some was pilfered and taken home. There was dancing, horseplay, and even some fighting. I chose to say nothing to my dad or the managers about any of this. Following my coworkers' lead, I, too, began to eat from the large pots of soup or the fried chicken that was pulled out of the frialator and participated in their mischief. Now they had something on me. It was then that the seed of trust was sewn.

Over time, the distrust melted away, and I became part of their world, no longer an outsider. They finally accepted me. Weeks and months passed, and I was receiving the life lessons of a Black person firsthand. During these moments, I studied their culture, dialect, habits, rituals, beliefs, and fears. Not long into my tenure, I talked more like they did, listened to their music, and acted as they would, emulating their personalities. The time served at the cafeterias provided me valuable lessons about their lives and challenges. What I learned was that every day was uphill for the Black employees. They had it hard. I became a witness to their everyday challenges trying to make it in a White-dominated world.

The workers and I eventually become closer, and I was invited to parties, we hung out together, and I was proud to call my Black brothers and sisters friends. This despite warnings from my dad to avoid getting involved with "the help." Dad wasn't prejudiced by any means but said this as good advice from his management perspective. His counsel wasn't heeded.

Grappling with Moving Forward

As years passed, I fondly remember my time at the cafeteria and the wisdom gained from being around my friends, "in the back." Time traveled on, and I was transported back to the White bubble I came from simply due to environmental forces that played out. But I didn't forget. It seems I always had a passion for the underdog, and my Black brothers and sisters definitely fit that description. Taking these lessons learned in my teens, I tried to hold sacred the equality we shared back at the cafeteria. It was hard since most of those around me and those who I grew up with still harbored prejudice in some form. This pressure chipped away at my beliefs over time, and I found myself sometimes slipping back into some bad habits. The pressures were all around me but didn't discourage my interest in Black lives. As one of my electives in college, I took Black American literature, studying W. E. B. DuBois, Frederick Douglass, Malcom X, and others. We were taught about the many horrendous crimes during the time of slavery and even in the modern era. This uncovered events we should know about Black history and we, as a White race, have a great deal to be ashamed.

When we're not around the Black culture, we tend to lose perspective about how they're treated. If we're not in it, we don't know it. My affinity for having Black and Hispanic friends never wavered. I sought out relationships and tried to cultivate trust that was always so very hard to earn. Sometimes it worked; other times it didn't.

Time has flashed by, and now that I'm retired, there are fewer and fewer opportunities to interface with Black colleagues I once had at work or to develop friendships outside my limited sphere of exposure. Hopefully God will create more opportunities to commune with people of color in the future.

EXPAND FORUM

One day it happened. Linda, our Sunday school leader, who is White and has a Black son-in-law, issued a challenge to our class to do something about racial injustice. Picking up the phone, I called Pastor Montreal Martin, who was a Black pastor at Wheatland United Methodist

Church in Dallas. Wheatland was founded back in the mid-1800s and is a Texas historical landmark. My great-great-grandfather was one of its founders. Having familiarity with the church and knowing it was in a predominantly Black neighborhood, I decided to call Pastor Monty to set up a forum to discuss racial issues. A few weeks passed, and a group was assembled of like-minded Christians, and we began discussing the injustices happening around the country.

The Zoom calls were named the "Expand Forum" by Pastor Monty, and they covered a lot of territory. We listened to videos with Black presenters, had guest speakers, and discussed ways to improve relations. The calls were successful and left the impression that we've begun to bridge the gap. We're nowhere near the place we need to be—yet. But it has to start somewhere. Some of the things I learned from my time at the cafeteria still hold true regarding today's race relations. First, I've learned that Black folks will never completely trust White folks. Even when my friends and I were close at the restaurant, there was always a shadow present. It was a faint shadow of uncertainty that hung over the relationship. The injustice the Black race has been subjected to by their White counterparts make it extremely difficult to earn complete trust. Second, Blacks and Whites are distinct people. White individuals will never understand what it feels like to be in a Black person's shoes, so we shouldn't act like we can relate. We just can't. Similarly, our Black friends can't step into our shoes and relate to the "White programming" we've been subjected to and reinforced over many generations. It hasn't been an easy task for White individuals to shed the negative indoctrination instilled by our forefathers. No matter how sincere we are as White people, we must constantly struggle with our pasts and the inheritance of prejudice. This White problem is scarcely comparable to what Black folks have experienced, but it should be made known for complete understanding.

From a Black Perspective

There are occasions when I watch my White brothers and sisters take special pains to be politically correct and overly cordial to accept Black individuals. This type of excessive flattery or pandering is transparent and can insult the intelligence of our Black brethren. They should be treated as we would treat any White person. Nothing more, nothing less. A response that turns off a person of color is when a White person says they don't see color. "Everyone is the same to me." This is an important lesson learned from the forum. Black individuals do not want to be seen like every other color. They want to be seen and known as Black individuals with all the proud heritage it represents.

White individuals should also be aware that Black folks don't mind being called Black. Many Whites, for some reason, are hesitant to call Blacks, Blacks for fear of it being considered an insult. When first meeting Pastor Monty, I tiptoed around the term and used the description, African American. Soon it became obvious that Black was the correct term to use, and we shouldn't be afraid to call a Black man a Black man. There's minor resentment when Blacks are presumed to be African Americans, meaning they're born with a direct lineage from Africa. Some blacks are not; they're from Caribbean or Central American bloodlines for example. That's why the preferred term is Black.

There are certain terms that are offensive to Blacks, even though it may seem trivial to a White person who wouldn't think twice about using the word or phrase in the presence of a person of color. These elicit visions of slavery. It may seem apparent that words such as "chains," "bondage," "slaves," "whip," "hanging," and "noose" should be avoided in normal course of a conversation. But we can easily find ourselves saying, "I've been chained to my desk," "I took a whipping over that," or, "He's a rebel." Typically a black listener will graciously overlook the unintentional insensitivity, but it registers nonetheless.

Diversity Is Beauty

There will always be differences between races, and we shouldn't overlook these. We should celebrate diversity. An important fact will always remain, God loves everyone the same. The minor difference of skin color shouldn't be a factor in our lives. Color is not important to Him, so why should it be to us? If we are to emulate God's love for our fellow humans, it should include everyone, not limited to those who look like us. All races should be sensitive to each other's beliefs and appreciate where we've come from and our respective ancestries. It would behoove us all to make stronger efforts to bridge the gap between races and avoid being conspicuous and exaggerated. Take every opportunity to speak to, communicate with, and relate to someone who is not of the same race. Show love; hold out the hand of peace. Let's get rid of racism.

> A lie doesn't become truth, wrong doesn't become right, and evil doesn't become good, just because it's accepted by a majority. (Booker T. Washington[102])

Dear Lord, bring us all together, and guide our understanding. Help us to celebrate color and diversity. Lead us to be one. Amen.

AFTERWORD: THE RECKONING

As we draw to a close and read the final words within the confines of the beginning and ending pages, we can conclude that *nobody* is a nobody to God. Each individual created in His image has the same currency value. The Lord has a penchant for the humble, the downtrodden, the ill, the aged, those discriminated against, and those who have little, but have other treasures to offer.

Worshipping God is not for weaklings. The question we should ask ourselves is whether we're strong enough and tough enough to battle the demons lurking in the shadows. Do we have what it takes to be a devout Christian? This challenge is for you, for me, and for everyone who desires eternal life. No one ever said this road to faithfulness would be painless. We can either follow the wide, unending road jammed with lost sheep or make our way through the narrow gates leading to paradise. Eternal life depends on our decision.

In the preceding chapters we found out how vital optimism and a positive attitude are to our faith and overall health. Conversely, we learned how detrimental worry, stress, and anxiety can be to the relationship with our Creator, not to mention our own mental well-being. We should engage our patience dynamic and become hyperaware of our moments of pride. The challenges of dealing with difficult people and practicing forgiveness were also emphasized as part of God's formula for spiritual maturation.

I'm a Nobody's objective is to help us understand our relationship with God and learn ways to establish communication lines with our Maker. The messages contained herein purposely accentuate how essential it is to *do something* and help our fellow man. We should escape our comfort zones, and find how rewarding these efforts can be. We should eliminate doubt and gossip along with any other imperfections we've developed. We've had a glimpse of miracles, heaven, and everlasting life as well as the darkness that awaits those who don't heed the Lord's commands.

Before parting we should acknowledge the importance of the church and supporting its activities heartily and generously. Finally, to make our best efforts to improve our relations with those who are different from ourselves and foster growth to become brothers and sisters in Christ.

While writing this book I could feel God at the controls as the words were composed, chapter by chapter. I thank Him humbly for the insight and enlightenment He's provided along the journey. Thanks be to God for everything He's given us, especially the ability to strengthen our faith and bolster efforts to emulate Jesus.

Dear Father, I pray that these words will be broadcast to those who need guidance and to use these concepts to grow closer to You. We are reminded, even nobodies can be somebody to You. Amen.

ACKNOWLEDGMENTS

I'm a Nobody could not have been written without the life lessons collected from all those who have helped me on my faith journey. Each person provided a torch to follow and led me to where I stand today. Whenever my devotion to God flagged, there was always someone who changed my course and rekindled the flame. These friends and family have challenged me to be my best, which sometimes fell short of God's design. But I'm confident He has forgiven me for my shortcomings. The Lord knows my heart.

Without my wife Sue's dedication to her faith and my spiritual development, I wouldn't be clicking the keys at this moment. To her, my heartfelt thanks and eternal devotion. We made this journey together with God's blessing. It's only proper to honor my mother who passed away some time ago. She is my inspiration today, thirty years after she left this earth and went to join the new kingdom. Jean Hasty instilled religion into my being whether I knew it or not at the time. It was a seed she planted when I was a teen. It's my hope that she'd be proud of the tree that's grown from the seeds she sowed, nourished by her strong belief in Jesus Christ. Mom, I love you. My sister, Celia

Hasty Carter, has been my companion as we both explored religion. I can't thank her enough for her family leadership and undying love for the Lord. Thank you, Dad, for all the life lessons. You were a strong yet quiet leader and a bounty of wisdom. Peace be with you, Wilton Herbert Hasty.

An important shout out to my son Nick Hasty and his wife, Melanie. Nick and Melanie are fervent in the Lord and a daily inspiration. Their strength and faith in Jesus are unparalleled, and it's certain they are on the path of righteousness. God bless you both. To my daughter, Natalie Hasty Harris, her husband, Will, and my son Neal Hasty, I pray often that someday you will all accept Christ into your lives. I'm comforted knowing that you are all Christians in your own ways. To my brother, Wil Hasty, I pray that you too, will someday come to know the Lord. It's never too late. Lastly, to my grandchildren—Lily, Luke, and James—who have embarked on an early path walking with God, I'm so proud of you three.

I thank the following individuals for their support and direction, good counsel, and wisdom. Many are clergy and past clergy of St. Andrew United Methodist Church in Plano, Texas. My gratitude goes out to Reverend Robert Hasley, our church leader and champion for Christ; teaching pastors Scott Engle and Lauren Gerlach; Senior Pastor Arthur Jones; Reverend Allison Jean; Reverend Jimmy Decker; Reverend Jennifer Arnold and Reverend Kim Myers for the leadership they've displayed. Each has helped lead our church and its expansion into the many hearts that crossed the sanctuary threshold. I would also like to show my appreciation to Reverend Janet Collinsworth for igniting my passion for missions and Reverend Debbie Lyons for welcoming me to St. Andrew many years ago. Thanks also to Reverend Edlen Cowley and the late Reverend Charles Stokes for their dedicated service to the church and Father God. Blessed are the sounds from Josh Miller and his soul mate, Krista, along with members of their band who bring God into focus with the sound of their music at St. Andrew.

Appreciation goes out to my family members, most of which are no longer with us. A few of these ancestral Methodists carried the family torch to where it is today. Love and thanks to the late Samuel and Elanor Branson Uhl, founders of Wheatland UMC the late Tom Brixey and Carrie Lee Uhl; the late Claude and Eula Bogard; the late T. J. and Dot Turner; Dick and the late Sue Flournoy; Bill and Ann Howsley; the late Mack and Minnie Mae Bogard; Stephen and the late Margaret Griffin; the late Wilton and Florence Hasty and the late Richard and Mary Jo Hasty.

Other family members to thank for their undying love: Michael and Pam Jurlina; Jacob and Anna Jurlina; Sabrina Jurlina; Michael and Jerri Peiffer; Jan Hasty; Mark Carter; Justin and Kathy Carter; Steve and Debbie Spangler; Wes Spangler; Jeff and Roxie Spangler; Brian and Ashley Bulte; Al and Jennifer Pierotti; Kirk, Pat, Ian, Noah, and Zac Pierotti; Tom Vehr; Jenny Vehr; Andy Vehr; Jeanne Hambleton; Brian Hambleton; Matt and Te'Aira Hambleton; Brittany Estrada; Hailey Hambleton; Jack Hambleton; Garrick and Michelle Hasty; Autumn Hasty; the late Bella Hasty; Brendon Hasty; Alura Hasty; Adelyn Pierce; the late Bobby Joe and Birdie Helton; my late mother-in-law, Ruth Hargett and her late husband, Bob Hargett: my father-in-law, Dick Vehr; and Sue's oldest sister, who passed away far too early in life, Judy Pierotti; Al and Cindy Pierotti; Roy and Pam Marchbanks and Matt and Lori Marchbanks. Lastly, the late Eldon and Betty Conrad. Eldon, we miss your righteous prayers before meals. And Betty, we miss your delicious cooking at our family get-togethers.

The writings in this manuscript were a result of presentations to the St. Andrew UMC's Seekers Sunday school class. I've had the honor of sharing this information, which was inspired by the members of our class for whom I have deep appreciation. I'd like to thank Brent and Deny Branham; Bill and Debbie Brewer, whose leadership at St. Andrew has changed the lives of many; Linda Buteyn; Mike and Shirley Castaneda, both kindred spirits of the arts; the late Kay Cavin; Pete Den Boer, the best meat smoker in town, and his wife, Arlyce; Reid and Luann Dolly, our mission and travel buddies; Helen and Duke Dupre; Susan Eeds; Ann Farris; Jo Ausley and her late husband Boyd; concert buddy Dennis Gilmore; Dennis and Pam Guth; Elden and Nancy Hale; John and Peggy Hamm; Susan Hauser and her late husband, Larry; Jon and Kathy Henson; Mel McGyver and his wife, Linda Samuel; Don and Barbara Myers; Sharon Neal; Jodell Oakley; Dale and Sharon Ochs; Janet Olivia; Larry and Linda Rivera; Velvet Schultz; Sharon Schroder and her late husband, Larry; Mary Kay Schultz; Karyl Stewart; Dwight and Karen Sumner; Linda Waldo; Mike and Kathy Waters; Melynda Swann; Phil Young; Dean and Nancy Kudich; West Texas confidant Jerry Rimes and his wife, Carolyn; Sandra Smith and her late husband, Clyde, who brought scripture to life; Craig and Marcie Taylor; Drew and Charlotte McKinney; Micah Mahaney, fellow alum of Carter High School, and his wife, Pam, who are both tireless servants of the Lord; and Pat and Kathleen McMahon for their service to our Bible study classes and to the Something Else Class.

Thanks go out to fellow church soldiers of grace: Candace Winslow; Matt and Jessica Lowe; fellow Carter alum, Kay Richardson; Jeff and Jordan Wonsmos; Reverend Steve and Connie Robertson; Rachel Kortum; Michael Agnew; Patti Engle; Sharon Hasley; Taylor and Ashley Whitlock; Jason Kimm; and Reverend Doug Myers.

My deepest appreciation goes out to the friends we met at St. Andrew over the years who have enriched Sue's and my life. Grab N Go meal service stalwart, Mona Carpenter; Pat Gageant, who taught us the beaded cross-making business; Gary and Jan Brooks, committed servants of Christ to those in need; Greg Wood, dear friend of travel and mission with a heart as big as Texas; Guy and Stephanie Burgoon, who helped us get our feet on the ground at St. Andrew; Rich and Cindy Flora, who assisted us entering into mission service and who remain strong supporters of those less fortunate; Bill Warren; Lisa Moreland; Mike Thatcher; Carolyn and Elbert Getridge; Hal and

Nancy Kurkowski; Rhonda Sanchez; Mike and Gayle Zak—Gayle, your cooking still astounds me; Ned and Jeanne Montgomery; Tish Cessna, our music and mission buddy; Ray and Carol Carlton; Steve and Becky Horne; deepest respect for Amir Shafiei; Joe, and Laura Rule; Drake and Melanie Goolsby; Chris Derrett; Janie Morse- a Wheatland UMC alum; Len Wilson; Mike Algermissen; Paul and Kay Myers; John Horan; Forrest Pool; Jonathan Gregoire; Taylor Davis; Angela Williams; Holly Blais; Kyle Focht; Joaquin Aguliar; Cecil and Sara Taylor; Sandra Shaw; Janis Browning; Laura Clegg; Karen Sutherland Slotterback; the late Ken Walgren and his wife, Kay; Carter alum, Glen Potter; Eric and Amanda Marchand; Cid Smith; Ron and Defae Weaver; Ken and Donna Melton; Mike Morton; Molly Saturino Jester; Nancy Ellis; Vijay Kanaparthy; Ron and Leisa Barger; Lisa Test; Bill and Vici Herr; Creighton Gerlach; Louise Stokes; Charlie and Elizabeth Daigle; Heidi Bryan; Jennifer Hayes; Jill Jururd; Jim and Lonna Atkins; Jan Hevey; Joe McPherson; Sara Jones; Kathleen Smith; Kimberly Stewart; and Adam and Kelly Shoenfelt. Also to Ann Kline, my high school English teacher at David W. Carter and member of St. Andrew. I credit lessons learned in her class as my maiden voyage trying to figure out this confounding language of ours.

    I offer heartfelt thanks to my brothers and sisters at Custer Road United Methodist Church. This mission-minded congregation has supported the health-care mission in Matamoros called Juntos Servimos for many years. It was founded by my friend Larry Cox and his wife, Nancy Rodriguez Cox. This forward-thinking couple built and operated Casa Bugambilla, a refuge for the sick, homeless, and broken. It also focused on educating the youth of Matamoros. The facility was built over several years from the ground up with volunteer labor and contributions from dedicated supporters. Through their efforts, hundreds of people were given hope and healing, both physically and spiritually. Juntos has been an instrumental chapter in the pilgrimage of my growth as a Christian. It was in Matamoros that

I first felt God tugging on my shoulder to help others. It was because of Larry's and Nancy's undying devotion to help those less fortunate, my life was changed forever. It's impossible to properly express my gratitude other than to keep your mission energy alive in whatever I do. Larry, Dr. Nancy, I've learned so much from the two of you and will try to emulate your passion. God bless each of you.

The leadership of Custer Road's mission team was exemplary, and I thank Ellen Curnes; Dave and Jennifer Wagner; John and Suzanne Gajdica; Stephanie Mills; Michelle Buffham; Chad and Janine Townes; Heather Hammer; Brian Scheibmeir; Becky and Gib Dawson; and Debra Black. Debra, I've never heard prayers so eloquently spoken. You have a gift of expression that assures me God is listening. Thanks also to our longtime friends David and Debbie Pomponio. A special tribute is offered up for Geoff, Christy, and Rebekah Hart, the Custer Road family who lost their lives in the tragic car accident mentioned in chapter 7. Additional thanks go to Highland Park United Methodist Church members and leaders who supported Juntos Servimos, Frank and Linda Roby, as well as vital contributors of time and resources, Dick Gozia and David Miller.

The acknowledgments would be incomplete without showing gratitude to my close personal friends from junior high and high school. One is Clyde McCray and his wife, Schantile. Clyde, you've always been there for me, and I'm blessed that we could reconnect in a more active way later in life. I've been friends with my concert buddy and confidant Bill Aicklen for nearly fifty years. His strong faith and righteousness have inspired me to seek higher ground amid the world's chaos. Thanks to faithful companions, Rocky and Ruthann Saldana; Don and Randi Taylor; Gary and Vickie Roark; and Jim and Bonnie Beishem Harlow. Bonnie, you're the most optimistic person I've ever met, and your faith has no equal. You're a bright star in the night sky.

Good friends from Carter High School who are immersed in the Lord, thank you: Gay Robinson Murray and her late husband and good friend, Pat, as well as their mission-minded daughter Meghan Murray. Thanks also to Larry and Dana Froese Krouse; Mark Frankie; Brad Shumate; Lucy Flach Allen; and Elsie McGinnis Smith. Your faith is inspiring. And I also send thanks to Reverend Len McLaughlin; Warren Hattersley; and Bob Acuff.

While establishing a career, I was fortunate enough to meet wonderful people I consider soulmates. First, I'd like to thank Cam Lindsey and her husband Jordan. Cam, we had a lot of enjoyable moments in our finance career over the years and survived many battles and challenges, most of which made us stronger and more successful. I have a deep respect for you as an individual as well as a leader, mother, wife, and generous friend. I'm also grateful to know and to have worked with a gentle soul and devout Christian, Deri Ward. Thanks to my friends Shawn Goffinet and his dear wife, Sara, as well as Dayna Smith and her husband, Ryan. Shawn, Dayna, as representatives of the younger generation, I find hope in the future of our country's faith. You're both inspiring to watch and assure me that the younger generation still has champions of God. Thanks for serving as role models.

Those I've worked with over the last four decades have strengthened my perseverance and Christian beliefs: Craig Cunningham and his wife, Sarah; Robert Johnson and his wife, Wilson; Pat Trainor and his wife Donna; Stephen McPherson; Sherri Owen; the late David Obergfell; Nancye Patterson; Phil and LeeAnn Gatlin; Gary and Susan Jones; Melissa Scott; Mark and Cindy Gonzalez; Robert and Reverend Sheron Patterson; Makia Epie; Tom and Grace Garcia; Ashia Cook; Regina Velasquez and Cedric Powell. Also friends Beverly Green and Tom Crabb. Love you all.

Dr. John Tolson, it's hard to express my sentiments. Your inspirational leadership over the years as host of *The Gathering of Men* lunches and the weekly *Red Glasses Talks* has made a serious impact on my life. Your straight-talk, no frills counseling has helped our family and our walk with Christ. There are a select few who I consider a mentor on my journey with God, and you're found at the top of the list. Thanks for your enduring passion and energy for leading men to know Christ. Appreciation also to my table mates at the *Gathering* who gave me support as we developed brotherhood: Doug Mulvihill, Johnny Martinez, Kit Haltom, Steve O'Neal, the late Al Aicklen and Wacyf Ghali. Wacyf, your friendship has been important to me in learning how fortunate we are to worship freely and to be thankful for the many blessings we have in America. Thanks for your unique perspective on Middle Eastern faith.

It's my belief that Mother Teresa has been reborn in the form of my beloved friend Lilliana Rojas. Lilliana works tirelessly to improve lives, spiritually, physically, and intellectually in her native country of Costa Rica. Her background in medicine has helped heal so many, and her strength in the Lord allows her to spend countless hours helping those in need and bringing them to God. Her passion is educating the youth, and Lilliana has established and implemented programs for young men and women to receive an advanced education while simultaneously teaching them the importance of faith. Lilliana, it's been a privilege knowing and working alongside you through The Eagles and the Serving by His Grace ministries over the years. You are an inspiration to everyone you meet. Dios los bendiga.

I'd like to recognize others that have worked with Lilliana on various projects within the Serving by His Grace alliance, especially Haydee Matarrita, who is the spiritual leader for the ladies in several Costa Rican villages who make crafts and beaded crosses. The crosses can be seen at church, worn by a number of St. Andrew members. Also the throngs of women who showed up early one morning, walking several miles to meet the St. Andrew mission team to learn crafts. They were so eager to learn trades and find a way to support their families. It was amazing to watch these Costa Rican ladies take a tiny shred of knowhow and grow it to heights no one could ever have imagined. I have the deepest respect for each of you and your work.

To the young men and women of the programs Lilliana has established, I want you to be aware that my faith has grown from knowing you. It might seem that you were the benefactor of the missions, but let me assure you, Sue and I gained as much from the endeavors as you have. Thank you Abraham Vasquez; Aaron Matarrita Portuguez; Eddy Solis; Jeyner Gutierrez; Danny Diaz Jimenez; Johanna Gomez; Jocelyn Fernandez; Jenniffer Araya Fonseca; Jose Ilder Diaz; Harold Casco; Esnyader Vasquez; Ashlyn Gonzalez; Harrison Vasquez; and Laura Grijalba. I'd also like to thank the mothers of The Eagles who wanted nothing more than to better their children's futures. Blessings to Hellen Jarquin; Mayra Gutierrez; Jahayra Rosales; Angela Elizabeth Casco; and Emily Matarrita Portuguez. A special thank you to the late Don Isidro, the patriarch of the Naranjal village, who donated his land to build a church and medical clinic in Naranjal. These fortifications are a lasting memorial evidencing your generosity. Don, I know you're in heaven sitting next to Jesus. Also to Pastor Valentine in Jabuy, located in the Talamanca Mountains in southern Costa Rica. His generous donation of land to St. Andrew made the building of Clinica Emanuel possible in the remote mountain villages of the Cabecar Indians. God bless you, Pastor. Other Costa Rican brothers and sisters in Christ that I'd like to thank are Fernandez Noré; Daniel Cordoba Sanchez; Dr. Black; Luis Lazo; and Sergio Hernan Bobadilla Munoz.

Sincere thanks to our dear friends Mark and Lyn Asbury. Our longtime friendship has enhanced Sue's and my life as individuals and as a married couple. You two are the blueprint for a successful marriage. Also our thanks to your wonderful children, Kerri and Kip. The combination of your mature faith and side-splitting humor makes life fun when we're with you. God bless the two of you. To our many friends, neighbors, and companions, we offer our best to Towfik Teherani and his late wife, Jane, whose faith could not be measured on earth, so God took her early in life; Munzer Adam, our extraordinary guide on our trips to Israel; Greg and Laura Hatch; Kyle and Amy Pierson; Robby Ogren; Bill Lintner; Craig Bess; Matt Nesrsta; Nick Daigle; Victoria Freudiger, my friend and first publisher; Mike McPherson; Evangelina Manzo, who has worked with our family for three generations; Billy Collinsworth; Dr. Jim Denison, author and publisher of *Denison Forum*; and Adrienne Nicholson and her staff at the Stewpot in Dallas.

I express deep gratitude to Reverend Janet Collinsworth and her undying efforts to help young women in crisis through the nonprofit she founded, Agape Resource & Assistance Center of Plano, as well as her role in the founding and support of the Costa Rican ministries. Between you and Lilliana there are no others I would rather work with to build a mission. Thanks to all the dedicated employees of Agape, especially Linda George, who has been a tireless beacon of light for the city of Plano as well as supporting the Costa Rican ministries.

Recently I met Pastor Montreal Martin, who served as senior pastor of Wheatland United Methodist Church in the Oak Cliff section of Dallas. We were brought together via the Expand Forum created to face the challenge of the continued discord between Whites and Blacks in our country. We were successfully able to establish dialogue and understanding through our joint efforts to gain an appreciation of our different cultures and ideologies. Not only has he enlightened a number of us at St. Andrew, Pastor Monty has introduced us to some mission projects. This includes the Grab N Go meal service and providing food to the needy through the North Texas Food Bank. Thank you, Pastor, for being a friend first of all, and for teaching me how to be more sensitive to my black brothers and sisters. It's individuals like you who will eventually bring the races together for lasting peace. God bless you.

I also thank members of the Expand Forum for their participation and input, especially Kathy Pryor and Kala Raglin. Props to Patsy Stephens, who is Pastor Monty's right-hand assistant keeping everything running smoothly. Love to Tonya Johnson; Stephanie Mitchell; Sabrina Peoples; LaTonya Humphrey; Lauren Antunez; Tony Antunez; Troy Mitchell; Michael Humphrey; Traci Mitchell; Dwayne Cook; Shacorya Mitchell, Demi Williams, David Batts, Tony Johnson, Shaun Oliver, Brendon Moore, Shatonia Mitchell, Melanie Mitchell; and Shadai Brinchfield for their efforts with Grab N Go. Melanie's husband, Virgil Mitchell, was lost recently to a battle with COVID, and I give tribute here to the quiet servant who served alongside the team. We miss you.

Recently two churches came together and shared Courageous Conversations. A Texas-sized thank you to the members of St. Luke's United Methodist Church in Dallas for helping those of us from St. Andrew understand more about how Black lives matter. Shout out to Ella Wright; Pastor Velda M. Turnley; Bonnie Warren; Deralyn White; Marian Williams; Eileen and Renaud Richardson; Fannie Smith; Dr. Janice and Donald Moore; Gary and Tracy Moton; Skylar Nunley; Alva Baker; Lorna Bormer; Carmen Guzman; Pam Mickens; Marion Solomon; Ed Moore; Marshall Hicks; Diane Moore; Gary and Helen Woods; Mae Rowlett; Judith Collins; and the leadership of Rick Hightower. May God continue to dwell within each of you.

Thanks to my little brother, Jovany Navarro, who I've had the privilege of meeting through the Big Brothers and Big Sisters mentoring program. Getting to know you has broadened my perspectives in many ways. Appreciation also to your mom, Veronica, and aunt Rosa.

Christian authors were instrumental in writing the passages of *I'm a Nobody*. Here's sending God's love to you whether on earth or in heaven: C. S. Lewis; Dr. Joyce Meyer; Dr. John Tolson; Dr. Rick Warren; Deepak Chopra; Sarah Young; Anita Diamant; William P. Young, Oswald Chambers; Bilquis Sheikh; Charles Colson, and Anne Frank. I'm sure there are others. Lastly, thanks to Father Tim Church for your teachings and leadership, Dr. William Rea for your groundbreaking strides in homeopathic medicine, and Dr. Ron and his late wife Chris Overberg for teaching me so much about health and nutrition.

The many individuals listed are the influences that brought the words to life in this writing. God led me through a maze of chance encounters with each person to set the stage for *I'm a Nobody*. The Lord undoubtedly used me to write His words because I *am* a nobody. But I am comforted, as always, knowing I'm not a nobody to God.

> The chances you take, the people you meet, the people you love, the faith that you have. That's what's going to define you. (Denzel Washington[103])

SOURCES

1. Watson, Galadriel. "Why some people are more optimistic than others—and why it matters." August 17, 2020. www.washingtonpost.com/lifestyle/wellness/is-the-glass-half-full-your-age-might-affect-your-optimism-but-the-pandemic-may-not/2020/08/14/ec8d52d4-d290-11ea-8d32-1ebf4e9d8e0d_story.html. Accessed January 31, 2021.
2. *Oxford Lexico.com.* nd. www.lexico.com/en/definition/hope. Accessed January 22, 2021.
3. *Oxford Lexico.com.* nd. www.lexico.com/en/definition/optimism. Accessed January 22, 2021.
4. Keller, Helen. "Helen Keller Quotes." *BrainyQuote.* www.brainyquote.com/quotes/helen_keller_164579. Accessed January 15, 2021.
5. "Helen Keller FAQ, Who was Helen Keller." *Perkins School for the Blind.* www.perkins.org/history/people/helen-keller/faq. Accessed January 15, 2021.
6. Bloom, Rebecca. "Rebecca Bloom Quotes." *Goodreads.* www.goodreads.com/quotes/203856-i-think-i-am-going-to-have-to-supercharge-my. Accessed January 15, 2021.
7. Morrow, Jonathan. "What Did the Jewish Historian Josephus Really Say about Jesus? 3 Things Every Christian Should Know About Josephus and Jesus." *Jonathan Morrow.* www.jonathanmorrow.org/what-did-the-jewish-historian-josephus-really-say-about-jesus/. Accessed January 15, 2021.

8   Robin, Dr. Michelle. "B. K. S. Iyengar on Health and Harmony." *Dr. Michelle Robin*. https://www.drmichellerobin.com/b-k-s-iyengar-health-harmony/. Accessed January 31, 2021.

9   Jackson, Mahalia. "Mahalia Jacson Quotes." *BrainyQuote*. www.brainyquote.com/quotes/mahalia_jackson_302645. Accessed February 3, 2021.

10 Armstrong, Brock. "How Exercise Affects Your Brain." *Scientific American*. December 26, 2018. www.scientificamerican.com/article/how-exercise-affects-your-brain/. Accessed January 31, 2021.

11 Armstrong, Brock. "How Exercise Affects Your Brain." *Scientific American*. December 26, 2018. www.scientificamerican.com/article/how-exercise-affects-your-brain/. Accessed January 31, 2021.

12 Okun, Dr. Michael. "5 Ways To Preserve Your Brain Power." *Spirituality & Health*. www.spiritualityhealth.com/articles/2016/05/17/5-ways-preserve-your-brain-power. Accessed February 21, 2021.

13 Vivekananda, Swami. "Goodreads Quotes." *Goodreads*. www.goodreads.com/quotes/238665-the-cheerful-mind-perseveres-and-the-strong-mind-hews-its. Accessed February 22, 2021.

14 Bonhoeffer, Dietrich. "Dietrich Bonhoeffer Quotes." *BrainyQuote*. www.brainyquote.com/quotes/dietrich_bonhoeffer_134459. Accessed February 22, 2021.

15 Voltaire. "Voltaire Quotes." *BrainyQuote*. www.brainyquote.com/quotes/voltaire_399778. Accessed February 7, 2021. https://www.facebook.com/240099582707854/posts/7-subtle-symptoms-of-prideby-fabienne-hartford-pride-will-kill-you-forever-pride/1012109832173488/. Accessed February 20, 2021.

16 *Oxford Lexico.com*. nd. www.lexico.com/en/definition/attitude. Accessed February 2, 2021.

17 Alder, Shannon L. "Pharmacy Quotes." *Pinterest*. www.pinterest.com/pin/195484440049531992/. Accessed January 24, 2021.

18 Young, L. F. "Quotable Quote." *Goodreads*. www.goodreads.com/quotes/1016303-don-t-hang-with-negative-people-they-will-pull-you-down. Accessed February 14, 2021.

19 "Zig Ziglar Biography." *Top Results Academy*. topresultsacademy.com/authors/zig-ziglar/biography/. Accessed January 4, 2021.

20 Ziglar, Zig. "Zig Ziglar Quotes." *BrainyQuote*. https://www.brainyquote.com/quotes/zig_ziglar_617769. Accessed January 17, 2021.
21 Ziglar, Zig. "Quotable Quote." *Goodreads*. www.goodreads.com/quotes/833302-life-is-too-short-to-spend-your-precious-time-trying. Accessed January 4, 2021.
22 Bhandari, Smitha, MD. "What Does Stress Do to the Body." November 17, 2020. www.webmd.com/balance/stress-management/stress-and-the-body#1. Accessed January 10, 2021.
23 Etkin, Amit, MD, PHD. "Brain Scans Show Distinctive Patterns in People with Generalized Anxiety Disorder in Stanford Study." *Stanford Medicine News Center,* December 7, 2009. med.stanford.edu/news/all-news/2009/12/brain-scans-show-distinctive-patterns-in-people-with-generalized-anxiety-disorder-in-stanford-study.html. Accessed January 20, 2021.
24 Caesar, Julius. "Julius Caesar Quotes." *BrainyQuote*. https://www.brainyquote.com/quotes/julius_caesar_125875. Accessed February 2021.
25 Young, Sarah. "Joy and Thankful Heart." *Jesus Calling*. joyandathankfulheart.wordpress.com/2015/06/07/i-am-all-around-you-like-a-cocoon-of-light/. Accessed January 31, 2021.
26 Yoder, Joanie. "Overcoming Worry." *Our Daily Bread*. https://odb.org/overcoming-worry-dsl/. Accessed May 25, 2021.
27 Coolidge, Calvin. "Calvin Coolidge Quotes." *BrainyQuote*. https://www.brainyquote.com/authors/calvin-coolidge-quotes. Accessed February 20, 2021.
28 Larry Eisenberg. "Larry Eisenberg Quotes." *Goodreads*. https://www.goodreads.com/quotes/532768-for-peace-of-mind-resign-as-general-manager-of-the. Accessed February 20, 2021.
29 Roger Babson. "AZ Quotes." https://www.azquotes.com/quote/576663. Accessed February 20, 2021.
30 Mignon McLaughlin. "Quote Fancy." https://quotefancy.com/quote/1321008/Mignon-McLaughlin-Love-looks-forward-hate-looks-back-anxiety-has-eyes-all-over-its-head. Accessed February 20, 2021.
31 Arthur Somers Roche. "Forbes Quotes." *Thoughts on the Business of Life*. https://www.forbes.com/quotes/789/. Accessed February 20, 2021.

32. Mary Carter Crowley. *Goodreads*. https://www.goodreads.com/quotes/199924-every-evening-i-turn-my-worries-over-to-god-he-s. Accessed February 20, 2021.
33. "Hypomone. Here's a Greek Word for Endurance You May Not Know—But Now You Will." *Glory Books*. http://glorybooks.org/greek-word-endurance-hypomone/. Accessed February 24, 2021.
34. "Hypomone. Here's a Greek Word for Endurance You May Not Know—But Now You Will." *Glory Books*. http://glorybooks.org/greek-word-endurance-hypomone/. Accessed February 24, 2021.
35. Graham, Billy. "10 Quotes from Billy Graham on Patience." *The Billy Graham Library*. September 3, 2018. https://billygrahamlibrary.org/blog-10-quotes-from-billy-graham-on-patience/. Accessed February 24, 2021.
36. Billy Graham Evangelistic Association. "Answers." January 18, 2014. https://billygraham.org/answer/patience-is-a-gift-from-god/. Accessed February 24, 2021.
37. Meyer, Joyce. "BrainyQuote." https://www.brainyquote.com/quotes/joyce_meyer_567645. Accessed February 20, 2021.
38. Hartford, Fabienne. "7 Subtle Symptoms of Pride." *TCF Abu Dabi*. October 22, 2015. Accessed February 24, 2021.
39. Lewis, C. S. *Mere Christianity*, 1942, 1943, 1944, 1952. Reprinted with permission. Accessed February 24, 2021.
40. Hartford, Fabienne. "Subtle Symptoms of Pride from Jonathan Edward, by Fabienne Hartford." *Church Leaders*. September 27, 2019. https://churchleaders.com/pastors/pastor-articles/263137-seven-subtle-symptoms-pride-2.html. Accessed February 24, 2021.
41. Marbaniang, Domenic. "Quotable Quote". *Wordpress*. https://marbaniangdomenic.wordpress.com/2016/01/27/the-opposite-of-love-is-pride/. Accessed February 24, 2021.
42. Barton, Bruce. "Quotable Quote".*Goodreads*. https://www.goodreads.com/quotes/95397-conceit-is-god-s-gift-to-little-men. Accessed February 24, 2021.
43. Franklin, Benjamin. *Quotes*. http://www.quotss.com/quote/The-devil-wipes-his-breech-with-poor-folks-pride. Accessed February 24, 2021.
44. Weiner, Herve. "Thoughts on the Business of Life." *ForbesQuotes*. https://www.forbes.com/quotes/4346/. Accessed February 20, 2021.

45 Kauflin, Bob. "Words of Wonder: What Happens When We Sing?" *desiringGod*. https://www.desiringgod.org/messages/words-of-wonder-what-happens-when-we-sing. Accessed February 10, 2021.
46 Kauflin, Bob. "Words of Wonder: What Happens When We Sing?" *desiringGod*. https://www.desiringgod.org/messages/words-of-wonder-what-happens-when-we-sing. Accessed February 10, 2021.
47 Unknown. "Music Brings Us Closer to God?" *The Hymnal Blog*, July 23, 2012. http://thehymnalblog.blogspot.com/2012/07/music-brings-us-closer-to-god.html. Accessed February 20, 2021.
48 Ghandi, Mahatma. *BrainyQuote*. https://www.brainyquote.com/quotes/mahatma_gandhi_121411. Accessed February 15. 2021.
49 Meyer, Joyce. "The Poison of Unforgiveness." *Joyce Meyer Ministries*. https://joycemeyer.org/everydayanswers/ea-teachings/the-poison-of-unforgiveness. Accessed February 22, 2021.
50 Caudle, Stephanie. "10 Reasons You Should Forgive Those Who've Hurt You." *Huffpost*. June 26, 2016. https://www.huffpost.com/entry/10-reasons-you-should-for_b_7672696. Accessed February 15, 2021.
51 Dickens, Charles. "It Was the Best of Times; It Was the Worst of Times," *Literary Devices*. https://literarydevices.net/it-was-the-best-of-times-it-was-the-worst-of-times/. Accessed February 20, 2021.
52 Engle, Dr. Scott. Bible Study Class, St. Andrew United Methodist Church. April 24, 2018.
53 Keller, Helen. "Helen Keller Quotes." *BrainyQuote*. https://www.brainyquote.com/quotes/helen_keller_120988. Accessed February 24, 2021.
54 Brenner, Abigail, MD. "5 Benefits of Stepping Outside Your Comfort Zone." *Psychology Today*. https://www.psychologytoday.com/us/blog/in-flux/201512/5-benefits-stepping-outside-your-comfort-zone. Accessed February 18, 2021.
55 Razzetti, Gustavo. "How to Leave Your Comfort Zone (for the Better)." *Fearless Culture*. https://www.fearlessculture.design/blog-posts/how-to-leave-your-comfort-zone-for-the-better. Accessed February 20, 2021.
56 What the Yerkes-Dodson Law Says about Stress and Performance. *Healthline*. https://www.healthline.com/health/yerkes-dodson-law. Accessed February 21, 2021.

57 Ghandi, Mahatma. "Inspirational Quotes." *Pinterest.* https://www.pinterest.co.uk/pin/405253666445846115/. Accessed February 10, 2021.
58 Warren, Rick. *Pinterest.* https://www.pinterest.com/pin/110478997089873557/. Accessed February 21, 2021.
59 Bergson, Henri. "Quotable Quote". *Goodreads.* https://www.goodreads.com/quotes/875145. Accessed February 12, 2021.
60 Tolson, Dr. John. Gathering of Men, University Park Presbyterian Church, April 27, 2016.
61 Meyer, Joyce. "It's Not That Complicated." *Joyce Meyer Ministries, Everyday Answers with Joyce Meyer.* https://joycemeyer.org/everydayanswers/ea-teachings/it-is-not-that-complicated. Accessed February 5, 2021.
62 Stanley, Charles. "Conscience vs. Holy Spirit." *Element Christian Church.* https://www.ourelement.org/blog/55-aaron/377-conscience-vs-holy-spirit. Accessed March 1, 2021.
63 Wellman, Jack. "Is Your Conscience the Voice of God?" *Christian Crier.* July 27, 2016. https://www.patheos.com/blogs/christiancrier/2016/06/27/is-your-conscience-the-voice-of-god/. Accessed February 10, 2021.
64 Shakespeare, William. "William Shakespeare Quotes." *Goodreads.* https://www.goodreads.com/quotes/21546-our-doubts-are-traitors-and-make-us-lose-the-good. Accessed February 10, 2021.
65 Fenyman, Richard. "Richard P. Fenyman Quotes." *Goodreads.* https://www.goodreads.com/quotes/33583-religion-is-a-culture-of-faith-science-is-a-culture. Accessed February 10, 2021.
66 Bloom, Susan. "The science of giving: Why it feels good to give back." *Jersey's Best.* https://www.jerseysbest.com/community/the-science-of-giving-why-it-feels-good-to-give-back/. Accessed February 20, 2021
67 Riestra, Juan. "The Science of Giving: Why It Feels Good to Give Back." *Jersey Best,* December 17, 2019. https://www.jerseysbest.com/community/the-science-of-giving-why-it-feels-good-to-give-back/. Accessed February 10, 2021.
68 Dickens, Charles. "Charles Dickens Quotes." *Goodreads.* https://www.goodreads.com/quotes/18876-no-one-is-useless-in-this-world-who-lightens-the. Accessed February 15, 2021.

69 "Giving Tuesday: 5 Health Benefits of Giving." *ThinkHealth.* https://thinkhealth.priorityhealth.com/giving-tuesday-health-benefits-of-giving/. Accessed June 6, 2021.
70 Anonymous. *BrainyQuote.* https://www.brainyquote.com/quotes/winston_churchill_131192. Accessed February 21, 2021.
71 Day, Dorothy. "Dorothy Day Quotes." *Goodreads.* https://www.goodreads.com/quotes/1286525-the-best-things-to-do-with-the-best-things-in. Accessed February 10, 2021.
72 Twain, Mark. "Mark Twain Quotes." *BrainyQuote.* https://www.brainyquote.com/quotes/mark_twain_121526. Accessed February 20, 2021.
73 Dial Hope. "You Brought Pavement?" *24 Hour Inspirational Messages,* May 30, 2015. https://www.dialhope.org/you-brought-pavement/. Accessed February 20, 2021.
74 Sproul, R. C. "Are Those Who Have Never Heard of Christ Going to Hell?" *Ligonier Ministries.* https://www.ligonier.org/learn/qas/are-those-who-have-never-heard-christ-going-hell/. Accessed February 10, 2021.
75 Velarde, Robert. "What about Those Who Have Never Heard?" *Focus on the Family,* January 1, 2009. https://www.focusonthefamily.com/faith/what-about-those-who-have-never-heard/. Accessed February 23, 2021.
76 Warren, Rick. "Rick Warren Quotes." *Inspirational Words of Wisdom.* https://www.wow4u.com/rickwarrenquotes3/. Accessed March 1, 2021.
77 "Angel Types in Judaism, Types of Jewish Angels." *Learn Religions.* https://www.learnreligions.com/angel-types-in-judaism-123835. Accessed March 1, 2021.
78 Beckler, Melanie. "Melanie Beckler Quotes." *Goodreads.* https://www.goodreads.com/author/quotes/6851715.Melanie_Beckler. Accessed March 1, 2021.
79 Balarie, Kelly. "10 Things the Devil Doesn't Want You to Know." *crosswalk.com.* October 8, 2015. https://www.crosswalk.com/blogs/kelly-balarie/10-things-the-devil-doesnt-want-you-to-know.html. Accessed March 10, 2021.
80 Longnecker, Dwight. "Laughing at Lucifer with Lewis." *The Imaginative Conservative,* February 1, 2015. https://theimaginativeconservative.org/2015/02/laughing-lucifer-lewis.html. Accessed March 15, 2021.

81 Lewis, C. S. *The Screwtape Letters,* 1942. Reprinted with permission. Accessed March 12, 2021.
82 Lawless, Chuck. "God's Mission Has an Enemy: 10 Facts about Spiritual Warfare." *imb Articles,* May 17, 2017. https://www.imb.org/2017/05/17/mission-enemy-10-facts-spiritual-warfare/. Accessed March 15, 2021.
83 Henry, Matthew. "MyBible." https://mybible.com/covers/444. Accessed March 15, 2021.
84 Solzhenitsyn, Aleksandr. "Aleksandr Solzhenitsyn Quotes." *Goodreads.* https://www.goodreads.com/quotes/1020045-if-only-there-were-evil-people-somewhere-insidiously-committing-evil. Accessed March 17, 2021.
85 Defoe, Daniel. "Daniel DeFoe Quotes." *BrainyQuote.* https://www.brainyquote.com/quotes/daniel_defoe_379807. Accessed March 17, 2021.
86 Moody, Dwight. "Dwight Moody Quotes." *Goodreads.* https://www.goodreads.com/quotes/668373-the-bible-will-keep-you-from-sin-or-sin-will. Accessed March 17, 2021.
87 Hamel, John. "Four Primary Types of Miracles They Can & Will Happen for You." http://www.johnhamelministries.org/miracles_four_primary_types.htm. Accessed March 17, 2021.
88 Burrus, Daniel, "Apollo 11 Moon Landing—Doing the Impossible." July 24, 2019. https://www.burrus.com/2019/07/apollo11-doing-the-impossible/. Accessed March 17, 2021.
89 Shaw, George Bernard. "George Bernard Shaw Quotes." *Successories.* https://www.successories.com/iquote/author/25/george-bernard-shaw-quotes/1. Accessed March 20, 2021.
90 Twain, Mark. "Mark Twain Quotes." *BrainyQuote.* https://www.brainyquote.com/quotes/mark_twain_103535. Accessed March 20, 2021.
91 Penkalski, Julie. "The Importance of Family Mealtime." *Family & Children's Center.* https://www.fcconline.org/the-importance-of-family-mealtime/. Accessed May 31, 2021.
92 Penkalski, Julie. "The Importance of Family Mealtime." *Family & Children's Center.* https://www.fcconline.org/the-importance-of-family-mealtime/. Accessed May 31, 2021.

93 Obie, Brooke. "Spiritual Benefits of Fasting." *Guideposts*. https://www.guideposts.org/better-living/health-and-wellness/5-spiritual-benefits-of-fasting. Accessed May 31, 2021.

94 Obie, Brooke. "Spiritual Benefits of Fasting." *Guideposts*. https://www.guideposts.org/better-living/health-and-wellness/5-spiritual-benefits-of-fasting. Accessed May 31, 2021.

95 Edgar, Jeremy. "3 Kinds of Idolatry." https://canadianbibleguy.com/2017/07/17/3-kinds-of-idolatry/. Accessed March 12, 2021.

96 Luther, Martin. "Martin Luther Quotes." *Goodreads*. https://www.goodreads.com/quotes/643925-whatever-your-heart-clings-to-and-confides-in-that-is. Accessed March 13, 2021.

97 Spurgeon, Charles. "Charles Haddon Spurgeon Quotes." *Goodreads*. https://www.goodreads.com/quotes/208663-nothing-teaches-us-about-the-preciousness-of-the-creator-as. Accessed March 13, 2021.

98 Warren, Rick. "A Powerful Key to Prayer." *Pastor Rick.com,* 5 Dec. 2016. https://pastorrick.com/devotional/english/praying-together-a-key-to-powerful-prayer. Accessed March 15, 2021.

99 Wright, N. T. "Sermon Quotes-Belonging." *The Pastor's Workshop*. https://thepastorsworkshop.com/sermon-quotes-on-belonging/. Accessed March 17, 2021.

100 Mathis, David. "Enjoying Jesus through the Spiritual Disciplines." *Habits of Grace.* https://document.desiringgod.org/habits-of-grace-en.pdf?ts=1456697851. Accessed March 12, 2021.

101 Luther, Martin. "Great Quote by Martin Luther That I Thought I'd Share." *Reddit.* https://www.reddit.com/r/Reformed/comments/c1s6oj/great_quote_by_martin_luther_that_i_thought_id/. Accessed March 10, 2021.

102 Washington, Booker T. "Booker T. Washington Quotes." *Goodreads.* https://www.goodreads.com/quotes/9580325-a-lie-doesn-t-become-truth-wrong-doesn-t-become-right-and. Accessed March 20, 2021.

103 Washington, Denzel. "Denzel Washington Quotes." *Quotefancy.* https://quotefancy.com/quote/1460066/Denzel-Washington-The-chances-you-take-the-people-you-meet-the-people-you-love-the-faith. Accessed March 2, 2021.

CPSIA information can be obtained
at www.ICGtesting.com
Printed in the USA
BVHW061136150322
631520BV00001B/63